Beachcomber's
GUIDE TO THE
NORTHEAST

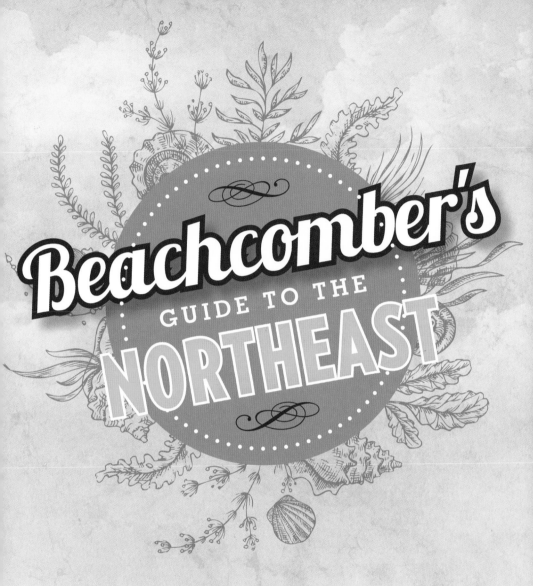

Beachcomber's
GUIDE TO THE
NORTHEAST

DAN TOBYNE

Down East Books

Published by Down East Books
An imprint of Globe Pequot
Trade Division of The Rowman & Littlefield Publishing Group, Inc.
4501 Forbes Boulevard, Suite 200, Lanham, Maryland 20706
www.rowman.com

Unit A, Whitacre Mews, 26-34 Stannary Street, London SE11 4AB, United Kingdom

British Library Cataloguing in Publication Information Available

Library of Congress Cataloging-in-Publication Data

Names: Tobyne, Dan.
Title: Beachcomber's guide to the Northeast / Dan Tobyne.
Description: Camden, Maine : Down East Books, 2016. | Description based on print version record and CIP data provided by publisher; resource not viewed.
Identifiers: LCCN 2015051411 (print) | LCCN 2015050829 (ebook) | ISBN 9781608934041 (e-book) | ISBN 9781608934034 (paperback : alkaline paper)
Subjects: LCSH: Beachcombing—New England—Guidebooks. | Beachcombing—Atlantic Coast (New England)—Guidebooks. | Beaches—New England—Guidebooks. | Beaches—Atlantic Coast (New England)—Guidebooks. | New England—Guidebooks. | Atlantic Coast (New England)—Guidebooks.
Classification: LCC G532.5.N49 (print) | LCC G532.5.N49 T63 2016 (ebook) | DDC 910.914/60974—dc23
LC record available at http://lccn.loc.gov/2015051411

Printed in the United States of America

Contents

Acknowledgments

'd like to thank my friends and family for the time they spent with me along the shore; also, Eric Alexander and his son Ean, for their companionship on my numerous extended coastal excursions; Catherine Racer, for her assistance with editing ("Yes, Kate—Strunk and White"); my editors, Mike Steere and Stephanie Scott, for their help and patience; production editor Meredith Dias and copyeditor Melissa Hayes for creating order out of chaos; and all the others who offered assistance and encouragement along the way.

The author, far right, during an early trip to the beach.

Introduction

> I seem to have been only like a boy playing on the seashore,
> and diverting myself in now and then finding a smoother
> pebble or a prettier shell than ordinary, whilst the great ocean
> of truth lay all undiscovered before me.
>
> —*Isaac Newton*

When I was a child, I loved everything about the beach: the sand, the salty air, the cold, damp concrete leading to the breakwater stairs, the sun in all its blazing glory forever attempting to peel the skin from my shoulders and nose, and the flotsam and jetsam the waves cast upon the shore, arousing my adolescent curiosity. Most of all, though, I loved the shells and other drift-line booty left for the taking: skate-egg casings, goose-fish teeth, slipper shells and angel wings, calcified horse mussel shells and sand dollars—all gifts from the sea. This was the magic the beach held for me, and each day's tide was a new experience. I knew the tide went out and at some point came back in, but it did so on a different schedule than mine, for each morning when I visited the beach, the tide would be in a different place.

It wasn't until much later that I understood the science behind what was happening. The moon, and, to some degree, the sun, exert a gravitational pull on the Earth that has its greatest effect on our seas, pulling them up into a bump of uplifted water as it passes below. And because the moon takes extra time to travel around the Earth, the tides are fifty minutes later each day. Although this seemed a nuisance when I was young, I decided I could live with the inconvenience, just as long as the tide continued to eventually show up and drop off stuff for me to explore.

Some beaches also leave tide pools behind, a special gift for the curious beachcomber. Tide pools are nature's touch tank, and, unlike the ones found in aquariums, you never know what you might find at the beach. I loved exploring tide pools as a child; it was the ultimate game of hide-and-seek, and I played it with great concentration. I admit it was unfair at times, since I often employed the most sophisticated scientific equipment of the day: a magnifying glass, dip net, mason jar, and the ultimate secret weapon: my trusty black high-top sneakers—PF Flyers—because they "helped you run faster and jump higher," allowing me to move swiftly from one spot to another, unimpeded by the barnacles that held sentry duty on almost every stone. It was just plain fun to explore these micro neighborhoods of the land between the tides.

For a long time my favorite environment was the beach of my youth, Long Beach, in Rockport, Massachusetts. Bordered by a seawall running the length of the beach, it's also anchored on both ends by rock outcroppings—the pinkish-brown granite that covers much of the coastal Northeast. It was and is a sandy beach nestled between two other beaches. To the left lies Cape Hedge Beach. Mostly cobbled, it was once known as Popple or Pebblestone Beach. To its right and just around the corner is Gloucester's Good Harbor Beach, one of that city's most public beaches. The water at Long Beach—so named because it's the longest beach in Rockport—is crystal clear, and, I've always believed, the coldest water anyplace in the world, receiving no aid from the Gulf Stream to bring its temperature up above what feels like the freezing point.

Long Beach, like many other Cape Ann beaches, has had its share of shipwrecks. In 1902, a British tramp steamer named *Wilster* landed on the beach after first grinding on some rocks in the shoal waters of Thatcher's Island. Eventually hauled off the beach, she was repaired and went on her way. The refloating of the *Wilster* attracted much attention, but the shipwreck that's always intrigued me and helped fuel my youthful exuberance is the wood-framed wreck at the southern end of the beach. She shows herself infrequently these days, usually after storms, and I'm often told she's the remains of a boat named *Surprise* out of Wiscasset, Maine. However, I've always chosen to believe otherwise; for me this ribbened set of shiply bones was further evidence that pirates roamed along this coast, burying treasure for me to find.

My youthful dreaming was all about pirate treasure, and as I poked and searched through the sea lettuce and bladder wrack, I dreamed of finding a map or a few coins— any sign of buried gold.

As I've grown older, I'm still looking for treasure, but treasure of a different kind, and whether collecting or stacking beach stones, looking for sea glass and pottery shards, or just walking the tidal shore, the rhythm of the sea, the changing breeze and slowly moving sky, sometimes makes me pause. In that moment a door opens, allowing me the opportunity to step inside myself, gather my thoughts, and see the world in a different way. I still look down at the water's edge, searching and hoping as the sea foam recedes that I might find a coin or a nugget or two, but I'm also searching for something lost—a map of sorts to an inner treasure, to inner peace—a place where I can calm the stress and ever-increasing velocity of life in the twenty-first century.

Only in the last few hundred years have we removed ourselves from this intimate type of relationship with nature, a relationship that we as human

beings have nurtured throughout our evolutionary development, and are just now beginning to rediscover. There's something to be said for the healing powers of the blue-green sea and the correlation between these magic colors and the reduction of stress, anxiety, and depression in our lives. The German poet Rainer Maria Rilke once wrote: "When anxious, uneasy and bad thoughts come, I go to the sea, and the sea drowns them out with its great wide sounds, cleanses me with its noise, and imposes a rhythm upon everything in me that is bewildered and confused."

The sea has offered this to me throughout my life, and I have tried to take advantage of it as I continue to examine the emotional wrack and seaweed of daily life.

The Beach

My dad and I used to call each other "beach buddies." We kids grew up on the beach, but for many years after college, when my brother and sister weren't living close, and I still had summers off, he and I would wake up early, drive to Nauset, just the two of us, and spend the day at the beach together. We would talk, read, dance, listen to music, and collect all sorts of things along the shore. I loved it. It's one of my fondest memories of my youth, and time spent with my dad.

—*Caitlin R.*

New England has more than five thousand miles of coastline with beaches that come in all shapes and sizes. There are pocket beaches, sand beaches, headland, barrier and cobbled beaches, beaches dwarfed by giant dunes and others by granite cliffs, flat beaches, steep beaches, mud, peat, and clay beaches, beaches strewn with stones of all sizes, and others, blankets of sand. From Greenwich, Connecticut, to Eastport, Maine, there's an endless

possibility and variation of sea and sand, each with its own unique and different signature, like fingerprints, defining their place along the shore.

But even with all the unique and different looks a beach can have, there
are still only four basic beach types: pocket beach, barrier beach, mainland
beach, and spit. *Pocket beaches* are those found between two headlands and look
very much as the name describes, although they can vary remarkably in size,
shape, and composition. *Barrier beaches* start and end in the water and move
with the shifting sand, sometimes becoming attached to the mainland and
sometimes looking more like an island. *Mainland beaches* are linear, attached
to the mainland, and make up a large number of the world's beaches. They're
usually part of a complex ecosystem that includes sand dunes, salt marsh, tidal
flats, and lagoons. *Spits*, or bars, as they're often called, are connected to the
mainland at one end, and end in the ocean at the other.

All beaches are shaped by wave action and ocean currents, and can contrast sharply with each other even in close proximity. Sand, Pemaquid, and
Jasper Beach are all pocket beaches in Maine. Sand Beach in Acadia National
Park on Mount Desert Island is composed of 40 to 70 percent shell matter,
a rare sand for a cold-water climate. In contrast, Maine's Pemaquid Beach to
the south, located on the Pemaquid Peninsula, is made up predominantly of
quartz eroded from nearby granite outcrops, giving this beach a bright, white,

fine-grained appearance broken only by the black mica that can be seen in its drift lines. In contrast to both of these beaches is Jasper Beach in Machiasport, to the north. Jasper Beach is composed of rounded and polished volcanic rocks of various sizes creating a high, elevated half-moon berm that has the appearance of slowly moving inland.

All this variety can be attributed to the last great ice sheet that descended over New England about twenty-one thousand years ago. A mile thick in places, it moved slowly over the region, rearranging the land as it ground off the tops of the Appalachian Mountains, scoured granite bedrock, and pulverized rocks and other material. Creeping at glacial speed, this enormous mass of ice dragged and tumbled displaced material and debris as it moved slowly southward, forever altering the landscape.

During this period, much of the Earth's water was locked up in this ice sheet, and ocean levels were much lower than they are today. Some scientists estimate that prehistoric sea levels were three hundred feet lower than they are today, creating a coastline sixty to eighty miles farther to seaward, and exposing a significantly larger area of the Atlantic coastal plain. If this is true, much of Cape Cod Bay was part of the mainland, and ancient islands existed along Stellwagen Bank. It also would have been possible for ancient peoples to walk from the mainland to Martha's Vineyard and Nantucket without ever getting their feet wet.

Evidence of this can be seen at Odiorne Point State Park in Rye, New Hampshire, where the remnant of an ancient forest is sometimes exposed at low tide. When this happens, white pine, hemlock, and cedar tree stumps— some up to eight feet in circumference—can be seen among the rocks and sand. Carbon dating estimates these forest remains, commonly called the "drowned forest," to be more than 3,500 years old.

As the ice began to melt, sea levels rose, altering the size and shape of the coastline. The retreating glacier, depositing large amounts of till and debris at random, created the drumlins, moraines, kettle ponds, and eskers that are now the features of present-day New England. Cape Cod, Martha's Vineyard, the Elizabeth Islands, and Nantucket were all created as part of this debris-ridden outwash plain, and mark the farthest advance of this massive ice sheet. As the glacier crept southward it picked up large, sometimes massive boulders that it dropped at random around the countryside; Doane Rock in Eastham, Agassiz Rock at Manchester-by-the-Sea, and the many rocks littering Cadillac Mountain on Mount Desert Island are classic examples of these boulders, known today as *glacial erratics*.

The finer particles of pulverized rock washed down to the sea, becoming part of the seabed. Transformed by the effects of wave, wind, and local currents, this weathered and eroded material is what we call sand today.

A beach is never static but always in motion, changing all the time. The beach we see today isn't the one we saw yesterday, or the one we'll see tomorrow. Each hour, each minute, each second, things are changing; sand is moved, creatures are coming and going, sandbars are slowly being constructed or dismantled, and objects are continually being placed or removed along the shoreline. Waves, constantly pounding the shore, continue to roll in seemingly

from a never-ending line of waves, all positioning themselves to have their turn at the shore, although this is an illusory vision, as waves are only a manifestation of the wind.

Waves are created by energy from the wind, building in a circular motion far out to sea. As they approach shallow water, the back side of the wave begins to drag on the ocean floor, forcing the remaining wave energy forward, building to a crest until the forward arc of the wave breaks, pounding the shore. As the energy dissipates, some of the water filters through the sand while the rest rolls back to the sea. High-energy waves seen in winter and during storms usually create erosion, pulling sand from the beach. Fairer-weather and less-energetic summer waves often cause accretion as they deposit new sand.

Most of New England's sand is made of ancient material; only the strongest minerals survived the process of decomposition. Quartz and feldspar, two of the hardest and most stable minerals, are the predominant components of New England sand. These two elements—along with other, more localized and newly eroded materials, such as shell fragments, hornblende, iron, and mica—give each beach its unique characteristics.

Two other natural events contribute to the ever-changing landscape: the wind, and longshore drift. The *wind*, whether onshore or off-, carries the finer grains of sand either landward, creating those beautiful sand dunes we often

see, or to seaward, reuniting the smallest and oldest grains of sand with the ocean's floor. The stronger the wind, the larger the particles it can move. The other phenomenon is called longshore drift.

Longshore drift is the movement of sand along a beach parallel to the shoreline. Sand is usually pulled off the beach at a 90 degree angle by a combination of energy, water, and gravity, but it's impossible for these three elements to place sand onto a beach in the same way. When a wave approaches shallow water and begins to drag on the bottom, increased friction allows it to pick up grain particles of sediment. Since no wave approaches the beach in a straight line—and rarely, if ever, at a 90 degree angle—the accumulated sand particles are moved sideways either up or down the beach as the wave breaks. Over time, this constant action of wave energy can move whole sections of sand, from one spot on the beach to another. Longshore drift, along with erosion or accretion, is the action that moves sandbars and shoal areas from one place to another, constantly altering the shape of things.

The Drift Line

Every time we walk along a beach some ancient urge disturbs us so that we find ourselves shedding shoes and garments or scavenging among seaweed and whitened timbers like the homesick refugees of a long war.

—*Loren Eiseley, American anthropologist, educator, philosopher, and natural science writer*

My favorite season to explore a beach is late fall, but any time of year is an adventure. The *drift line*, that stretch of sand where both man-made and natural materials accumulate, is usually my first stop, giving me an idea of what might be in store for me during my visit. Things collect in the drift line because wave energy isn't strong enough to pull them back to the sea,

or wind and water have combined to push things onto the beach that can no longer be reached by the breaking waves. Whatever the reason, all beaches have a drift line. Some beaches have more of a drift line than others, and sometimes, more than one.

The highest line of debris on a beach usually marks the storm tide or spring tide. A *spring tide* doesn't have anything to do with the season that follows winter. The term refers to the tide that "springs up" or "jumps" up the beach the farthest. This happens when a full moon aligns with the sun and their combined gravitational pull creates the highest tide possible. The drift line with the most seaweed and debris usually marks the spring-tide line.

We often find large amounts of seaweed on the beach. When it's alive in the water, seaweed "ocean algae" comes in many shapes and colors, but once on the beach, it's usually black, pungent, and, for many, unsightly and unwanted. Municipalities spend a great deal of time and money removing this kind of drift material, although its removal is not allowed on some beaches because its organic benefits can play a significant role in beach stability. It's also the initial substance nature provides for island building.

As kids, the best use my buddies and I found for seaweed was squirting each other while popping the bladders of knotted wrack, but only when we weren't busy chasing girls around with large pieces of ocean kelp.

All seaweeds, whether green, red, or brown, are members of the algae family, contain chlorophyll, and depend on the sun for their energy. Rockweed, also known as sea wrack, is a brown algae even though it looks green at times. When dislodged by a storm or other weather-related activity, it often washes up on the beach. Other common brown algae you'll see are sausage seaweed, cord weed, and various types of kelp. The two most common green algae I've seen in New England are sea lettuce and sea staghorn—more commonly known as dead man's fingers, or green fleece. I seem to notice red algae most often in the winter months, including bushy red seaweed, Irish moss, and dulse.

Driftwood, salt-marsh hay, dislodged peat, and other base materials are also commonly found in the drift line. Most, if not all, of this "debris" is considered a nuisance by beachgoers, but for the animals that call the beach home, it's a source of protection and food supply, and it plays a vital role in a beach's circle of life.

There are many items that wash up on a beach that most beachgoers find interesting and valuable. Seashells, sand dollars, sea urchins, and skate eggs, as well as polished stones and sea glass, are often considered by many to be gifts from the sea.

Many beaches have more than one drift line. Whether the beach is being eroded or built up, the elevation of the beach face and the size and shape of the beach's berm all contribute to the placement of material. Often many

shells and other collectibles can be found in the alternate drift lines, and, if you're a collector, you should be sure to comb all of these areas, because those things usually disappear with the coming tide. One day the beach is filled with oyster shells; the next day, they're gone.

There was a time when almost all the material found in the drift line was organic, but mankind is always leaving its mark, and today there is an increasing amount of man-made material washing up on our shores. Plastic items can travel thousands of miles either on or under the ocean's surface, and, because it degrades very slowly, it eventually ends up on the beach. We are also leaving a larger footprint as our population increases and more people crowd the shoreline.

Beach Creatures

No aquarium, no tank in a marine land, however spacious it may be, can begin to duplicate the conditions of the sea. And no dolphin who inhabits one of those aquariums or one of those marine lands can be considered normal.

—*Jacques-Yves Cousteau, oceanographer*

The beach is filled with unbounded life and, in a basic and fundamental way, is the place of our birth. As much as we are inventors constantly creating and building, driven to expand and change our environment, we also yearn to be part of the natural world.

The following is a short list of some of the more interesting and unique animals I've encountered on my travels to the beach. It is in no way a complete list; I'm not even sure what a complete listing of beach creatures would look like.

HARBOR SEALS

Andre the seal is probably New England's most famous harbor seal. Raised by a Mainer named Harry Goodridge, Andre was the subject of books and movies, and entertained visitors from all over the globe. He summered in Rockport, Maine, and wintered in aquariums—usually the New England Aquarium in Boston—and was famous for his swims home to Rockport each spring. Andre died in 1987 after entertaining millions for twenty-five years. A statue in his honor is located in Rockport, Maine, at the small public park near the harbor landing.

A short boat ride outside most New England harbors will bring you to some of the harbor seal's favorite haunts. There are about ninety thousand harbor seals living along the New England coast, and if you meet one on the beach, the encounter is hard to forget. They can grow to about six feet in length and live about thirty years. The best place to see harbor seals along the Maine coast is just about anyplace. In Massachusetts, you're sure to see seals if you visit the town of Chatham on Cape Cod. For many years now a colony of harbor seals has taken up residence on Monomoy Island, and on the sandbar just across the harbor from the town's main beach.

My most intriguing encounter was at Cape Cod's Head of the Meadow Beach during an early-morning fall hike. Just as I summited the dunes, there before me was a large group of seals bobbing in the water just off the beach. I said hello and they all began to groan at me. I'm not sure if they wanted me to do something or if they were just complaining about the weather, but they bobbed around, moaning and groaning, for the better part of an hour.

WHALES

Whales, like seals, are mammals, protected today after being one of the most exploited creatures on earth. Whaling in America initially consisted of locating dead whales on the beach. There were so many whales off the New England coast that at least three or four washed up each year. Refining whale blubber started out as a cooperative effort with different factions, including Native Americans, sharing in the process. As demand grew, a more active system was put into play, employing a couple of different techniques. When a large whale was sighted, small boats would be launched to harpoon and bring the whale back to the beach. When schools of smaller pilot whales, commonly called "blackfish," were observed, boats would be used to herd as many as possible to a location that would strand them. Blackfish Creek in Wellfleet, Massachusetts, got its name from the large number of pilot whales that met their demise there. It was not uncommon even into the twentieth century to see townsfolk hurrying down to the Creek to stake their claim to part of the school.

As the demand for whale oil increased, larger boats with the capability of rendering blubber on board became the standard, and New England became the epicenter of the whaling industry. The discovery of oil in Pennsylvania signaled the beginning of the end for the whaling industry in America, but not before these magnificent creatures were almost brought to extinction.

Today, a new industry has emerged: Whale-watching, driven by our interest in understanding and observing these magnificent animals, now flourishes up and down the New England coast.

FIDDLER CRABS

Although they are aggressive toward each other, fiddler crabs live in colonies by the thousands and spend most of their time eating, digging, and mating. They are strange little creatures and look like they were created with spare parts that don't necessary belong on the same body. They have ten legs, eyes situated on long stalks looking a little like periscopes, and for the males, one very large claw and one smaller claw. They have the ability to walk in any direction but usually walk sideways, the males holding their large claw in the air, sometimes waving it back and forth when threatened. Females can eat using both claws, but the males can only eat with one, using the larger claw to attract mates. They're essential figures in marsh ecosystems, feeding on decaying plant matter and aerating the soil with their constant digging. Fiddlers also have a primitive set of lungs, making them semiterrestrial, allowing them to live on land for extended periods of time, as well as gills, for living in the water. If you happen to come across a colony, usually at low tide when they're out of their burrows, it can seem a little unnerving, as tens of thousands of these little one-inch creatures march in unison, sometimes making it look as though the ground is moving. It was actually comical for me when I attempted to photograph one. You need to get fairly close, and as I looked through the lens, this strange little creature, holding its very large claw in front of its face, was peering back at me with periscope eyes, posed as if listening to me as I begged it to stand still.

HORSESHOE CRAB

Horseshoe crabs are often called "living fossils" because they've been around for almost 450 million years. That's 200 million years before the dinosaurs. Mislabeled as a crab, this strange-looking, heavily armored animal, with its long, swordlike "tail," is more closely related to spiders and ticks. It has nine eyes—seven on the top of its shell that include two compound eyes, and two on the bottom near its mouth. It also has light-sensing organs located in its tail.

The horseshoe crab is often spotted transporting other animals around. Mollusks—usually slipper shells, barnacles, and algae—can often be seen taking a ride on the carapace, or shell, of this armored creature. It also plays an important part in the life cycle and ecology of the beach. Horseshoe crab eggs are an important food source for many of the other animals, including many seabirds. The horseshoe crab is not marketed as a food source for humans, but its unique blue blood plays an important role in biomedical research.

You can find the shells of this animal in the drift line—usually as a result of molting—but if you'd like to see live horseshoe crabs, the best time is at night during mating season—usually between the full moons of May and June in New England, when they migrate to the beach.

HERRING/ALEWIVES

When I was young, I spent a lot of time in Falmouth, Massachusetts, with my uncle Herb, a transplanted Mainer, who made part of his living on the Cape by clamming and fishing. In the spring, he'd take me to one of the beaches in East Falmouth, where numerous inlets allowed tidal access to Falmouth's "ponds." Great Pond, Green Pond, Bourne's Pond, and Eel Pond are ponds in name only. They're actually saltwater inlets that look a lot like watery fingers intruding into the landscape. Uncle Herb and I weren't there to fish, however; we were scouting. Great, Green, and Bourne's Ponds are all connected to cranberry bogs at their northern end that in turn terminate at small freshwater breeding ponds, for herring. Each day we'd sit by the breakwater, drinking coffee and watching the dark boil of herring schools moving back and forth in front of us, just off the beach, as they waited for the magic moment when the rise in water temperature would trigger their migration. Once the herring began to move, the passive part of our expedition was over. In a few days we'd be headed for the cranberry bogs to get down to the business end of catching fish. In an hour, we'd net enough of these ten-inch beauties to keep us busy for the rest of the day, cleaning them. Once we finally dressed them out, my grandmother would pickle them, storing enough herring in her preserve cellar to last an entire year.

The name *river herring* is a general term, used to describe two different fish species: the alewife and the blueback herring. River herring and alewives

are anadromous, meaning they hatch in freshwater and migrate to the ocean, the adults eventually returning to freshwater to spawn. They were once so plentiful that almost every navigable river in New England had a population of alewives.

Today, river herring stocks are depleted, and many states, including Massachusetts, Rhode Island, and Connecticut, have moratoriums on harvesting, but for anyone interested in observing their annual migration, there are a number of locations available for viewing.

The Damariscotta Mills fish ladder is a prime location in Maine to view the alewife run, both up the ladder in spring, and down the ladder in the fall. They also have a festival for each event. In October Damariscotta holds a Soup and Chowder Festival celebrating the downstream migration, known as the "Running of the Alewives," and on Memorial Day weekend in May, the town celebrates the Annual Damariscotta Mills Fish Ladder Restoration Festival. The festival is sponsored by the towns of Nobleboro and Newcastle, and the Nobleboro Historical Society.

It you'd like to view the spring herring run in Massachusetts, the following locations will give you the best opportunity.

Bournedale Herring Run, Bourne, MA: This is an artificial waterway built so the herring could enter at spawning time. Access is from Route 6, about halfway between the two bridges.

Mashpee River Herring Run, Mashpee, MA: A man-made herring run next to the Mashpee Wampanoag Indian Museum on Route 130.

Bell's Neck Conservation Area, Harwich, MA: A man-made herring run is part of this 250-acre conservation land. Take Route 28 to Depot Road to Bell's Neck Road.

Paines Creek Herring Run, Brewster, MA: This series of natural "fish ladders" is located in a pond near the Stony Brook Grist Mill. Access is from Stony Brook Road, off Route 6A.

GOOSEFISH

The goosefish is an angler fish, and also goes by the names all-mouth, molligut, and sometimes devilfish. But if there's a Latin term to describe this creature, it should probably be along the lines of *Pisces deformis formidilosus* (the ugly, scary fish). Its body is almost all head and mouth, with up to three sets of teeth angled inward, to help pull in its prey. This all-mouth is an indiscriminate eater, can eat prey almost as large as itself, and will pounce on anything that gets too close.

A goosefish often sits on the bottom, dangling its strange elongated dorsal spine in front of its huge mouth, waiting for the curious passerby to get within range, before it lunges forward in one rapid motion, engulfing its prey. It's been known to eat flounder, squid, lobster, loons, ducks, sharks, and anything else that crosses its path. If you like to fish in some of the quieter coastal waters, you might want to invest in a pair of steel-toed waders. The largest goosefish caught on rod and reel was caught in Perkins Cove, in Ogunquit, Maine, weighing in at 49.7 pounds.

STRIPED BASS

Striped bass are a true fish of the beach and are rarely found more than a few miles from shore. They're a migratory fish, breeding in freshwater, with primary spawning areas in the Upper Chesapeake Bay, and the Delaware and Roanoke Rivers.

Striper fishermen are avid anglers; as much work goes into selecting the place to fish as actually fishing. Fishing at dusk and at dawn usually brings the best success, but you still need to know where the tidal rips, currents, and sandbars are to have a shot at bringing home the big one.

Smaller bass migrate in large schools and are known as "schoolies," while larger fish travel in smaller groups and are the fish that anglers seek out. The largest striped bass are called "cows" because they're usually females. Owing to their importance to the sporting industry and value in the marketplace, fishing for striped bass is highly regulated in most states, both for size and catch limit.

THE MONARCH BUTTERFLY

Monarch butterflies—also known as milkweed butterflies, because they lay their eggs on the underside of milkweed leaves—live a fascinating life, and their story of survival is unparalleled. Monarchs migrate to central Mexico every fall to overwinter and lay their eggs before heading off, usually to northern Mexico, to spend their final days. It's the newly hatched population that heads north to the United States and Canada, although this group will never make it to New England. Along the way the females will lay their eggs and possibly make it to the Gulf Coast area before they die. The next generation hatching from this new group of eggs continues the journey, leapfrogging over their parents as they migrate north. This process continues and is repeated until the great-great-grandchildren of the original group finally arrive in the Northeast. During the summer months new generations of monarchs will hatch, lay eggs, live for about a month, and die, until the last generation hatches in the fall. This is the generation that will migrate to Mexico. Unlike the northern migration that acted like some strange relay team, the fall population of monarchs will make the entire trip before laying their eggs and wintering over. To accomplish this task, this last group of summer monarchs is physiologically different than all the others. They mature, but are in a state of reproductive limbo known as *diapause*. Unlike the previous generations—whose average life span was four weeks—this group will be able to live as long as seven months, making it possible for them to fly thousands of miles to lay their eggs.

BIRDS OF THE BEACH

Seagulls

There are lots of different birds that inhabit the shore, the most recognizable being the seagull. The word *seagull* is a generic term used to describe a group of gulls, the most common of which are the black-backed and gray-backed gulls.

The black-backed gull is the largest gull in the world. Aggressive and powerful, they dominate the beach and are considered the king of the species. They are scavengers and forage far and wide for food, including at landfills and dumps. There is a lesser black-backed gull, but they're considered visitors more commonly associated with Europe.

Gray-backed gulls, also known as herring gulls, are the quintessential seagull of the New England shore. They are the most familiar of all the gulls, and representative of what people mean when they say "seagull." Like the black-backed gull, they scavenge for food and are responsible for the familiar scene of seagulls squawking and diving around the stern of a fishing boat, fighting for an afternoon meal.

Sandpipers

The sandpiper is a small migratory bird familiar to most beachgoers, often seen running along the shoreline, moving in and out, in rhythm with the waves as it searches for small animals to lunch on. These quick-legged little birds are usually hard at work avoiding the surf as they chase down the little creatures they feed on. This group includes sanderlings, semipalmated sandpipers, and white-rumped and least sandpipers.

Snowy Owl

The largest North American owl is the snowy owl, which can sometimes be seen in winter, sitting in the dunes or high on a perch as it surveys the beach, looking for its next meal. They often sit motionless for hours, blinking only occasionally to focus in on something. They use their extraordinary eyesight to track and catch their prey. Snowy owls are migratory and live most of their lives in the Artic, occasionally visiting New England in winter. A good place to observe one of these magnificent birds is at the Parker River National Wildlife Refuge, located on Plum Island in Newburyport, Massachusetts. Plum Island is a barrier beach island and home to the 4,700-acre sanctuary.

SPECIAL PLACES
Hammonasset Beach State Park—Madison, CT

A great place to observe the fall migration of the monarch butterfly is at Hammonasset Beach State Park in Clinton, Connecticut. In 2000, the Meigs Point Butterfly Garden opened at Hammonasset to attract butterflies, including the monarch. The garden is maintained by the Friends of Hammonasset, and Meigs Point participates in the monarch tagging and tracking program. The garden is an educational centerpiece for naturalists, and provides a blueprint for homeowners who would like to create their own butterfly garden at home. The ocean boardwalk just off the beach is also a great place to observe monarch butterflies during their migration.

Race Point—Provincetown, MA

Whales

Humpback, fin, mink, and North Atlantic right whales migrate to New England's Stellwagen Bank each year during the summer season, and thousands of human visitors come to watch them. Provincetown is located less than five miles from the Bank's southern tip, and whales can often be seen in and around the town's north-facing beaches. Currents along the Race are swift and strong, and the depth just offshore drops off sharply, allowing whales and other marine mammals to cruise in, close to the shoreline.

Bring your binoculars—although you don't really need them—and sit at the beach (my favorite time is late afternoon). There's a good chance you'll see at least one whale, probably more.

Parker River National Wildlife Preserve—Newbury, MA

Owls / Waterfowl

The 4,700-acre Parker River National Wildlife Refuge is located on Plum Island, in Newburyport, Massachusetts, and has a diverse habitat that includes marshland, cranberry bogs, sand dunes, and barrier beach. Thousands of migratory birds flock to this sanctuary each year, including the snowy owl.

Snowy owls are birds of prey and can be spotted from November through May as they migrate from their homes in the northern polar regions of the Arctic to more southern locations. On any given day during the migratory season, large groups of "birders" can be seen with their large spotting scopes and tripod-mounted binoculars, surveying the landscape for this sometimes elusive, sometimes prevalent, noble bird. However, anyone willing to make the trip has a good chance of spotting one without any viewing equipment at all. But if you don't, you're sure to see one or more of the other migratory bird species that pass through this special place.

Rachel Carson Salt Pond Preserve—New Harbor, ME

Although a tide pool is an unstable environment, it's a great place to find some of the interesting creatures that live in the intertidal zone. When the sea retreats, exposing much of the beach, it also leaves pools of water—trappings,

really, ranging from shallow puddles to large rocky ponds. The tide is the one constant in this otherwise harsh living space, requiring the plants and animals that live there to be tolerant of changes in their environment, including water temperature, changing salinity, the sun's rays, and a pounding surf.

One of the most dedicated observers of marine life was Rachel Carson. She spent countless hours observing the life of the intertidal zone at a special tide pool in Maine known today as the Rachel Carson Salt Pond Preserve. It's here that she did much of her work for *The Edge of the Sea*, her landmark book about marine life. The salt pond is part of Muscongus Bay and located between Waldoboro and New Harbor, Maine, along Route 32 at a small bend in the road. If you have a chance to visit this remarkable spot, consult the tide charts and try to arrive at low tide. You'll be able to explore the wonders of a classic Atlantic tide pool and observe nature in its natural environment.

Shells

Oh, tell the secrets thou must know
Of clouds above and waves below;
Oh, whisper of the bending sky
And ocean caves where jewels lie.

O beauteous sea-shell, tinged with red,
What dost thou know; what canst thou tell?
Unto what mysteries are thou wed,
Thou fragile thing, thou pearly shell?
A whisper of the sounding sea;
A sweep of surges strong and free;
A tale of life—a tale of death;
A warm, bright sin—an icy breath.
—*Fannie Isabel Sherrick, "A Shell"*

Seashells are the exoskeletons of invertebrate animals that, once empty, are left to the whim of current and tide, some eventually ending up in the drift lines and intertidal zones of the beaches we explore.

Over the years, shells have been collected and used for a wide variety of things. They've served as currency (wampum in New England), jewelry, buttons, musical instruments, bowls and utensils, hair combs, charms, brooches, even weapons. They've also been recognized as symbols in most religions, and are believed by some to have sacred powers.

One of the largest shell collections I've come across in my travels is located in Newcastle and Damariscotta, Maine, and what it lacks in diversity, it makes up for in volume. Tucked along the shore at a soft bend in the Damariscotta River are two large piles of shells, called *middens*—basically, shell dumps built over the millennia: the Whaleback Shell Midden on the east, and the Glidden Shell Midden on the west.

Indigenous peoples traveled to the seacoast to spend the summer months enjoying what the ocean and its surroundings had to offer. I guess you could say they were the first to discover the pleasure of summering along the New England shore, and like any good visitors, being respectful of nature, they tried to keep their refuse in one place.

The Whaleback Shell Midden was once the largest shell heap in Maine, measuring 30 feet deep and over 1,600 feet long, with an average width of 1,500 feet. Today it's much smaller, but it's still an impressive sight. The midden is predominantly composed of oyster shells, some dating back to 200 BC and measuring up to twenty inches in length, much larger than any oyster shell we see today. Over the years these middens have been exploited for different purposes. Much of the shell midden was ground up and used in chicken feed in the latter part of the nineteenth century, but in spite of this, there still remains an impressive display of shells now under the protection of the Maine Department of Conservation, which manages this historic site in cooperation with the Damariscotta River Association. If you're interested in visiting, you'll find it off Belvedere Road on US Route 1 Business / Main Street, in Damariscotta, Maine.

The shell middens were created long ago as a by-product of food gathering, and while some of the shells we collect today may also come by way of a similar process, the modern-day beachcomber is in search of empty shells, and prefers diversity over quantity. Some of my favorite shells to collect are oyster, scallop, angel wing, moon snail, jingle shell, jackknife, Stimpson's whelk, dogwinkle, and surf clam.

OYSTER

Oysters were a favorite food of indigenous people. They grew prolifically, covering so much of the harbors, bays, and inlets that they were often considered a hazard to navigation. Almost all the native oyster beds are gone now—a consequence of pollution and overfishing—and today's oysters (and oyster shells found on the beach) are usually from oyster farming. Today's oysters are the same oyster species, *Crassostrea virginica,* that originally inhabited local waters, brought up from the Chesapeake Bay and now farmed in New England waters.

You'll have good luck finding oyster shells on most New England beaches, but there are a couple places I found particularly interesting to visit.

Wellfleet, Massachusetts, made famous by Henry David Thoreau in his book *Cape Cod*, is considered by many to be the oyster capital of the

Northeast, if not the world. In 1605, when Samuel Champlain explored Cape Cod, he named Wellfleet Harbor "Oyster Bay." Each October the local citizenry celebrate the oyster at their Wellfleet Oysterfest, a three-day toast to their local economic engine.

If you visit the town of Wellfleet, don't miss the opportunity to take a short hike around the town's Cannon Hill Conservation Area. You cross Uncle Tim's Bridge over Duck Creek to get to Cannon Hill. Duck Creek was once a very busy place, and the center of oystering operations in Wellfleet. In 1870, when the railroad arrived, Duck Creek was cut off and most of the

activity was moved. If you decide to visit this quiet spot, you should walk over and investigate the remains of the train bridge. There you'll find oyster shells by the thousands. The area is saturated with them, and just to the left of the bridge, you should also be able see the remains of an old oyster boat sitting in the mudflats, covered with oyster shells. If you visit at low tide, you might be rewarded with another sight: Millions of fiddler crabs call this creek home, and they can be seen by the thousands, scurrying around the mudflats, doing whatever it is that fiddler crabs do.

Damariscotta, Maine, is home to the Damariscotta River and the ancient shell middens, and each year in September the town celebrates the oyster at the Pemaquid Oyster Festival. Today almost all of the oysters harvested here come from cultivated oyster beds, but over the years, as these cultivated oysters have spawned, oyster larvae have drifted downriver, developed, attached to rocks, old shells, and anything else they could find, and prospered. Wild oysters are back, at least in the tidal estuary of the Damariscotta River.

BLUE MUSSEL / RIBBED MUSSEL / HORSE MUSSEL

The Atlantic blue mussel is a native of the Atlantic Northeast and lives in the ocean's intertidal zone, attaching itself to rocks and other surfaces, using strong elastic strands known as *byssal threads*. The mussel's blue, purple, and sometimes brown shell is elongated, and its semi-smooth surface exhibits growth rings, allowing us to determine age. I've always been a fan of this shell simply because of its rich coloration. Blue mussels commonly live in mussel fields, but have been known to group together in clumps, possibly to aid in reproduction.

The mussel is a resilient creature and can live a long time in harsh environments—one of the requirements of the plants and animals that inhabit the intertidal zone. It can resist a wide range of temperatures and survive for extended periods of time out of the water by tightly closing its shell. Blue mussel shells are common on New England beaches, although sandy beaches tend to have fewer. My best luck finding these shells has always been north of Boston.

The ribbed mussel, the other common mussel found along the shore, prefers to live in tidal estuaries and mudflats, often partially buried in marsh banks and muddy creeks. They prefer a less-salty environment than their cousin, the blue mussel, and flourish in these back-beach areas because of the decreased salinity, caused by an influx of freshwater. Ribbed mussels attach themselves in much the same way as the blue mussel, using byssal threads secreted by their byssal gland. Ribbed mussels are filter feeders, and as they process organic nutrients, they create inorganic material as a by-product, helping to enrich the overall salt-marsh environment. Ribbed mussel shells aren't usually found on the beach unless the beach complex includes marshland, mudflats, and estuaries.

The biggest of all the mussels, the horse mussel, ranges on the Atlantic coast from Labrador to South Carolina, living just below the low-tide mark, to depths of one hundred feet. It can grow to nine inches in length, but in my experience, four inches is more the norm when finding these shells on the beach. Horse mussels usually form colonies, creating large beds that build up over time, becoming mussel reefs. These fields and reefs provide two services to the overall health of its aquatic biosystem: a protected space for other creatures to live, feed, and grow; and clean water. Five thousand horse mussels can filter up to 130 tons of seawater a day.

When you find these mussels on the beach, don't be surprised at the thickness of some of the shells. Mussels have the ability to thicken their shells as protection against perceived predators.

SCALLOP

Another of my favorite shells to collect is the scallop shell. There are two types of scallops in New England waters: bay scallops and sea scallops. Sea scallops live in deep ocean water. Their shell has a smooth radial surface pattern, and they can grow to about eight inches in diameter. Bay scallops, on the other hand, live in shallow water where eelgrass is present, and their shell looks quite different from that of a sea scallop. A bay scallop shell is fan-shaped with deep, defined ridges, and comes in a variety of colors: blue, white, brown, red, purple, yellow, and often, a mix of multiple colors. Bay scallops have a shorter life span than sea scallops, and their shells rarely grow more than three inches in diameter. Interestingly, they are the only bivalve mollusk that can swim. (*Bivalve* means it has two shells, or "valves," as they're called.) Using their strong abductor muscle, they expel water out of their shell and push themselves along, often in large groups. The best scallop shell collecting for me has always been on the islands of Nantucket and Martha's Vineyard, although I've also had good luck on many Cape Cod beaches, especially on the bay side.

ANGEL WING

How these delicate shells ever land on the beach in one piece is a mystery to me. The angel wing, false angel wing, and fallen angel wing—I confess, I usually can't tell them apart when I'm collecting—are also known as *piddocks*. They are another bivalve mollusk, and considering the fragility of these shells, it's amazing that these animals actually burrow into hard mud and soft rock surfaces, creating a hole to use as their living quarters. They

live longer than scallops, spending their entire life span of about seven years in the holes they create. When you find their shells on the beach, like scallop shells, they are seldom found together as a pair. But unlike scallop shells, they are usually white in color, which seems appropriate. After all, what other color would you expect angel wings to be?

The best spot I've ever found for collecting these shells is at the southern end of Crane Beach in Ipswich, Massachusetts.

MOON SNAIL

The moon snail is a beautiful shell. Its spire is symmetrical and colorful, and for me, a real treasure when found among some of the more-common shells. The moon snail is a carnivorous predator and feeds on surf clams, quahogs, and soft-shelled clams by drilling a hole into the shell of its prey, enabling it to reach in and consume its victim. You may notice shells on the beach

with a perfectly round hole. That's the work of snails, including the moon snail. Northern moon snails range as far north as Labrador. The lobed moon snail, sometimes called a "shark's eye" because of its bluish spire, is usually only found as far north as Cape Cod. Second Beach in Newport, Rhode Island, and Plum Island in Newburyport, Massachusetts, are good places to find northern moon snails.

JINGLE SHELL

Jingle shells, another bivalve, are small and, like oysters, attach themselves to objects to survive. The bottom shell is fragile and often oddly shaped, because it conforms to the surface it's attached to. What we usually find on the beach is the top half, or valve, of the shell. These small, thin shells are usually iridescent yellow and retain their beauty even when collected and dried. The shell gets its name from the sound it makes when they are shaken together. Because of their pleasing sound, jingle shells are often made into necklaces and wind chimes.

SURF CLAM AND QUAHOG

Two shells that are easy to find on most sandy beaches, including the colder waters of Maine, are the surf clam and the quahog.

The surf clam is one of the largest shells you'll find on a New England beach. They live in the sandy bottom of the coastal plain, from the intertidal zone of beaches to the deep waters of the continental shelf. These clams have a very thick shell and can grow to as large as ten or eleven inches. Also known as

a "hen" clam, their meat is often cut up and sold as clam strips in local restaurants. There was a time when almost every house in coastal New England had a surf clam shell as an ashtray, but today these shells, bleached white by the sun, are more often spotted in gardens or as seasonal decorations.

Quahogs are smaller than surf clams, and also go by a variety of different names, including little-neck, cherrystone, and hard-shell. They live in mudflats and just below the low-tide line, and their shells are usually found in abundance on most beaches. Quahogs are prized for their flavor. Smaller ones are usually eaten raw on the half shell, while the larger ones are used in chowder or in stuffed clams and clam cakes. Native Americans used the quahog shell to make beads that were originally ornamental, but became a form of currency (called wampum) when trading with Europeans. The most valuable part of the shell for currency purposes was the blue area of the inner shell; a blue bead had almost twice the value of a white one.

Both clams can live a long time in relation to other bivalves; the quahog can live up to twenty years, and the surf clam more than thirty years.

DOGWINKLE

The dogwinkle shell is a small snail shell, usually three-quarters of an inch to one and a half inches in size. It's rounded with a pointed spire, although it can look quite different at times, because growth development of this particular shell is affected by wave action and currents. Snails that grow in a sheltered space unaffected by strong currents can often have a rough exterior, in contrast to snails living in rougher waters that exhibit smooth shells. Dogwinkle shells are usually grayish in color but can also be black, orange, blue, or green. The shells can also be banded in various colors. A shell's color is partly determined by the snail's diet. A blue shell, for example, is a good indication that a particular snail was living on a steady diet of mussels.

Dogwinkles, or dog whelks, as they're sometimes known, spend their lives in the intertidal zone between the high- and low-tide marks. They can also be found in most tide pools. Like most snails, these small whelks are carnivores and feed on barnacles and soft-shell clams, drilling holes in the shells of their prey to gain access. Dogwinkle shells can be found on most beaches, and it's not uncommon to find large piles of these shells mixed with the shells of periwinkles along rocky shorelines.

COMMON PERIWINKLES / SMOOTH PERIWINKLES / ROUGH PERIWINKLES

The shells of littorines, commonly known as *periwinkles*, were the most common shell I found as a child growing up on Cape Ann, Massachusetts. Periwinkles are herbivores, and there's always been plenty of algae growing along the Northeast's rocky shoreline for them to feed on. There are three different types of periwinkles found in abundance in New England—the common periwinkle, smooth periwinkle, and rough periwinkle—and each species inhabits a different part of the intertidal zone.

The common periwinkle lives in the lower intertidal zone, grows to about an inch, and has a thick, smooth, brown or purple shell. The smooth periwinkle grows to about half the size of the common periwinkle, and can usually be found living and feeding on the rockweed that covers the rocks and other stationary objects in the tidal zone. Their shells are usually more colorful than the common periwinkle, often exhibiting a yellow or orange coloration. The third species, the rough periwinkle, lives in more-protected waters, and can be found in tide pools or hidden under rocks, in the upper portions of the beach.

JACKKNIFE CLAM

The jackknife clam is a filter-feeding bivalve found all over the Northeast. It lives in bays and estuaries that have sandy or muddy bottoms. Beachcombers will find many of their shells on the beach, but will rarely if ever see a live jackknife clam. Its slender, streamlined design allows it to burrow quickly when it feels threatened. Although it's an edible clam, it's seldom seen in the marketplace. This is because it can usually out-dig a clam digger.

The Atlantic jackknife is sometimes called a razor clam, and that's the name I've always used to describe it. But the term *razor clam* is actually used to describe another mollusk, and this is where things can become a little confusing: The Atlantic jackknife clam (*Ensis directus*), Atlantic razor clam (*Siliqua costata*), and the stout tagelus (*Tagelus plebeius*) are all called "razor clams" interchangeably.

WHELKS
Knobbed Whelk, Channel Whelk, Waved Whelk, Stimpson's Whelk

The *knobbed whelk* is the largest sea snail in the Northeast, and its shell is the largest treasure a shell collector will find on the beach. A knobbed whelk shell can range up to nine inches in length, followed closely behind by the channel whelk, at around eight inches. You can also find their egg casings if you know what you're looking for. Both whelks have casings that are parchment-like and elongated, held together by a string-like material. These often show up on the beach after the eggs have hatched.

A knobbed whelk has distinct knobs on its spire and a shell swirl that is almost always a "right-handed" coil, in a clockwise rotation. Shells with a counterclockwise coil have been found, but they are rare, so make sure you check all the whelks you find on the beach. A left-handed whelk is a valuable find.

Channel whelks, another predatory snail, has less-pronounced knobs on its spire and can grow to about eight inches at maturity. Both knobbed and channel whelks live in the low intertidal zone of beaches with sandy or muddy bottoms, and feed primarily on clams and other soft-shell bivalve mollusks. Both of these whelks are migratory, but don't usually range farther north than Cape Cod.

Waved whelks, on the other hand, range as far north as Labrador. This mollusk grows to about six inches, and its shell has a pronounced spire and raised body ribs. Where channel and knobbed whelks feed primarily on clams, the waved whelk is a scavenger that feeds on whatever it can find that's edible. This whelk can be found in the subtidal zone of beaches and also in deep water.

The *Stimpson's whelk* is smaller than the other whelks, grows to about five inches at maturity, and looks quite different from its relatives. It has more of a spindle shape and lives in depths of up to two thousand feet. This is another northern mollusk that can be found all along the Northeast, and even though it's a deep-water snail, Stimpson shells can often be found on the beach after a storm.

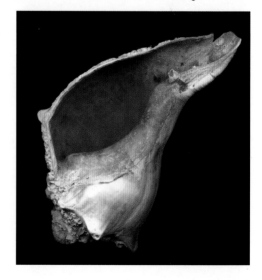

SPECIAL PLACES

Special shell-collecting beaches that have rewarded me with both volume and shell diversity are:

Silver Sands State Park Beach—Milford, CT

This beach is located on Silver Sands Parkway, Milford, Connecticut, and is open year-round. I was amazed at the number of shells on this beach, by the thousands. We found Atlantic slippers, eastern oysters, knobbed whelks, jingle shells, and dogwinkles, as well as skate egg casings and molted horseshoe crab shells.

Second Beach—Newport, RI

Second Beach is flat and sandy, and you can usually find surf clams, moon snails, and Stimpson's and waved whelks.

Brant Point Beach—Nantucket, MA

A scenic beach and the location of Brant Point Lighthouse (can't miss it coming in on the ferry), this beach is a collector's dream, with hundreds of multi-colored bay scallop shells and thousands of slipper shells, as well as many other species. My friend who spends a week on Nantucket every summer always goes to this beach to make a sailor's valentine—shells arranged in a special way, usually in a box as a souvenir or gift.

Falmouth Town Beach—Falmouth, Cape Cod, MA

This town is known for its plethora of south-facing beach jetties, which usually have plenty of jingle and slipper shells—great wind-chime material. Look around the jetties at the water's edge and you won't be disappointed.

First Encounter Beach—Eastham, MA

This sandy beach, located on Cape Cod Bay in the town of Eastham, will sometimes offer up clumps of oyster shells, some resembling unique works of art. One day they show up in the hundreds, and a week later, at low tide, all you'll see is sand. Part of the reason for finding these beautiful arrangements is probably the number of oyster farms located in the bay.

Wellfleet's Inner Harbor—Wellfleet, Cape Cod, MA

This beach has tens of thousands of oyster shells; go at low tide and visit the old railroad bridge.

Crane Beach—Ipswich, MA

Crane Beach is located at the end of Argilla Road and managed by the Trustees of Reservations. The beach is open year-round from 8:00 a.m. to sunset.

Some of my favorite shells from this beach are Atlantic slipper, Atlantic surf clam, jackknife, shark-eyed moon snail, dogwinkle, false angel wing, bay scallop, eastern oyster, Stimpson's whelk, Atlantic razor, and northern quahog.

Plum Island—Newburyport, MA

If there's one beach in New England that offers a diverse collection of shells and other drift-line treasure, it's Plum Island. Much of this barrier beach is located within the Parker River National Wildlife Preserve. Nearly one hundred different shell species have been found here, including gastropods (snails and slugs), bivalves, mollusks, and chitons; a small oval mollusk with a shell

resembling plated armor. Even a giant squid once ended up on the beach, eventually finding a home at the Smithsonian's Museum of Natural History. We've always had good luck here finding surf clams, starfish, sand dollars, quahogs, horse mussels, razor clams, and moon snails.

Seabrook Beach—Seabrook, NH
Seabrook Beach is sandy, and a good place to find shells, especially in the fall and early winter. I've found jingle shells, sea clams, and occasionally mussels, including horse mussels, along with slipper shells and the occasional limpet.

Rye Beach—Rye, NH
Rye Beach has a rocky spit with a number of tide pools that are great for shell collecting, but be careful of the rockweed; it's very slippery. You can find sea urchins, periwinkles, and the occasional limpet here.

Wallis Sands State Park—Rye, NH
This is a good place to find shells among the rocky sections. You can find bubbles, turret shells, winkles, and sea urchins in abundance.

Odiorne Point State Park—Rye, NH
This beach has lots of shells and is also home to the Seacoast Science Center. What I love most about this beach are the tide pools, lots of them up and down the beach. Some of the shells I've found here are arctic paper bubbles, arctic barrel bubbles, Noah's keyhole limpets, smooth top shells, dogwinkles, Atlantic periwinkles, and every other winkle you can imagine.

Beach Stones

Up in Maine where I have my boat there's an island with a long spit, covered in small stones. The waves break both ways over the spit, and those stones are polished as smooth as glass. The locals told me not to touch any of them—and definitely not to take any off the spit, because it's bad luck—but I'll bet you any amount of money every one of those lobstermen has one tucked away in one of his pockets for luck, hoping it helps keep him safe while he works on the water.

—*Chris C.*

Granite exists in abundance along the New England shoreline, and many of the stones and pebbles rolling around in the tidal wash are polished fragments of this igneous rock. Igneous rock is formed when existing rock is brought to the melting point deep below the Earth's surface and slowly cooled over time. This process forms a fairly homogenous material classified as plutonic, named after Pluto, the Greek god of the underground. Granite, which is an igneous plutonic rock, is only exposed after its softer rock covering is eroded away.

The different colors of granite are a result of different compositions of minerals in the stone. I'm fond of pink granite, and my favorite are the egg-shaped stones usually found on cobbled beaches. They're pleasing to the eye and have a balance and symmetry that fractured stones don't exhibit. Granite is extremely durable because of its high quartz content, making it a symbol of strength and longevity. Although not endowed with any form of life spirit, granite and other rocks and minerals have come to symbolize many different human emotions.

The Northeast played a significant role in the building of America, and New England granite—especially Maine granite—has helped symbolize the American spirit.

The US Treasury Building in Washington, DC, was built with Dix Island granite; the Brooklyn Bridge, with Vinalhaven Island granite; and the streets and curbs of Boston, with granite from quarries in Stonington, to name just a few.

Some people believe stones do contain a life force and are capable of absorbing and radiating vibrational energy. Whether this belief is based in truth or not, people have been carrying stones and using them as talismans and amulets for centuries. In ancient Egypt, one of the most popular amulets symbolized the heart. It was in the shape of a beetle and was carried for good luck. This might seem silly to some, but today, when we go to the beach and find a heart-shaped stone, who doesn't pick it up and put it in his or her pocket, or give it to someone as a symbol of their love?

Here's a little activity you might enjoy. The next time you go to the beach, find a few small milky-white quartz stones. Bring them to a dark place and rub them together. If you do this correctly, you should see light emitted at the point of friction, and the stones will glow. Although scientists don't fully understand what's going on when this happens, they say this phenomenon is caused by the breaking of chemical bonds, giving off electromagnetic radiation in a process known as *triboluminescence*, the result of an interaction between light and matter. Maybe for the sake of the child in all of us, we could just say it's magic.

Some people believe rocks contain metaphysical properties. Metaphysics is the study of the nature and dynamics of the universe and how all things relate to each other. Many people believe stones have the power to help with meditation, relationship building, communication, and many other aspects of our lives. One of these life stones is rhyolite, an igneous volcanic rock found in the Northeast. Rhyolite is considered the extrusive volcanic equivalent of compositional granite that cooled on the Earth's surface, not deep below ground. Crystal healing practitioners believe rhyolite has a strong life force with protective powers beneficial to the person who wears it.

Whether a skeptic or believer in the power of this stone, there's one beach in New England that is a must-see—Jasper Beach in Machiasport, Maine. Three-thousand-foot-long Jasper Beach is located at Howard's Cove in Machiasport, and is literally a giant stone dune. Most of the stones come from the eroding cliffs and headlands of this pocket beach that wave action has rolled smooth and storm action has thrown on to this crescent-shaped stone pile. The majority of these stones are red, brown, and green rhyolite, with some granite and quartz mixed in. The stones range from football size at the top of the pile to grain-size at the bottom, all polished to a smooth finish.

I can't speak to the protective powers of rhyolite, but lying on this rock pile after it's been warmed by an early-summer sun is better than any hot stone massage therapy I've ever experienced, as it relaxes muscles and melts away tension and stiffness. This, combined with the sound of ocean water receding through the stones as it travels back to the sea, is enough to make any skeptic a believer when it comes to the magic of Jasper's stones.

PUDDINGSTONE

Millions of years ago, large rivers dragged sediment and debris toward the Earth's ancient oceans, filling low spots in its path with large amounts of rock and silt. Over time this debris, built up and compressed by its own weight, solidified into what we today call *puddingstone*. Puddingstone is considered a sedimentary rock because it's a conglomerate of granite stones, other igneous rocks, and silt, fused together over time by massive amounts of pressure.

The best-known puddingstone conglomerate in the Northeast is the Roxbury Conglomerate located in and around Boston, Massachusetts; however, Rhode Island also has excellent examples, and there's a great display of this strange rock formation at Middletown's Second Beach. The stone formation runs under the road, exiting as a large outcropping near the western end of the beach. Further adding to this strange sight is the sea's ability to erode the softer silty "pudding" material, leaving the harder granite components protruding from the pile. When I first saw this as a child, I thought there'd been an accident during construction of an old seawall, and that the concrete and other material had somehow oozed onto the beach. Little did I know, it was all nature's work.

STACKING STONES

Today, it seems like everyone is stacking stones at the beach, and the volume of this effort tells me there's something else going on. It's not just something to do while spending time, enjoying the day. Stone piles, historically called *cairns*, were usually built for a specific function. They helped people stay on a path, ensuring that they could navigate a course of direction in places where the path was at times unclear. My first experience with cairns was in the White Mountains of New Hampshire on a particularly difficult section of hiking trail. It was almost impossible on that foggy day to know where I was, where I was going, or where I'd come from. These rock piles helped me stay on the path and avoid a potential calamity. Besides showing me the way, those stacked stones comforted me and allowed me to stay centered within myself. I knew where I was because I could see where I'd come from, and my path forward was clear.

Today, most of the writing about stone stacking explains the art of balance and people's ability as artist performers, designing innovative stone piles that seem to defy gravity. For me this explanation is only part of the picture. I believe people stack stones because, like me on that mountain many years

ago, it helps them find their center. It's a way of saying *Here I am*. I'm marking myself in this life journey, and nothing else matters while I'm doing this,

except my inner consciousness, as I work to blaze my life's trail. No, they're not built to last; it's the process that's important; otherwise, they'd simply be monuments to ourselves instead of an activity that assists us in marking our emotional existence, giving us the inner contemplation we need to understand where we've come from and where we're headed by helping us understand where we are. The next time you head to the shore for vacation, try stacking a pile of stones each morning, a new stack each new day. If you're like me, it might just help you stay on your path and find your way.

SPECIAL PLACES
Great Beach—Cape Cod National Seashore, MA

Quartz stones

I'm not smart enough to make this stuff up. All I know is that when you take quartz stones from the beach and rub them together, they give off light. The following has been excerpted from the *Cape Naturalist*, the journal of the Cape Cod Museum of Natural History, Vol. 24 (1997):

> [A] possible explanation [for this phenomenon] relates to the piezoelectric nature of quartz. Piezoelectricity is created when mechanical stress causes electrons within a crystal to flow, producing an electric current. Conversely, when a current is applied to a piezoelectric substance, such as quartz, the substance will deform and oscillate (vibrate) at a certain rate

or frequency. These characteristics allow the use of quartz in crystal phonograph cartridges (if you are a kid, ask a grown-up about the phonograph) or in quartz watches. Tapping or rubbing quartz pebbles together causes a mechanical stress within the quartz. The stress, in turn, causes an electric current to be generated within the pebbles. This current may ionize gases trapped within the quartz, producing the glow in the same way that current flowing between the ground and clouds in a thunderstorm produces a lightning bolt.

Winter Island—Salem, MA

Stone figures

Winter Island has an old fort, a lighthouse, and a seaplane hangar from its Coast Guard days, but I visit this place to look at the rocks. I'm not a geologist or rock hound, but I'm intrigued by the bas-relief and two-dimensional "stone creatures" on the beach's boulders, just below the fort. The fort is said to be haunted, and I once imagined these stone phenomena to be demons—malevolent spirits attempting escape. I suppose if I really wanted an answer I could look it up, or ask someone who understands geology, but what fun

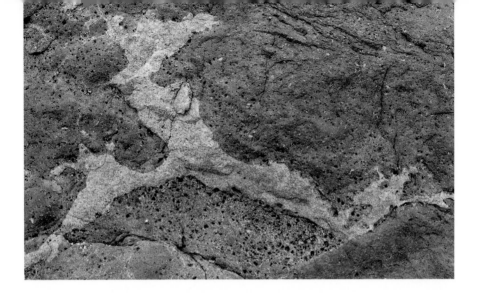

would that be? I think I'll just continue to let my imagination do the talking. It makes for a much better story.

Halibut Point State Park—Rockport, MA

For many years the Rockport Granite Company quarried granite at Halibut Point in Rockport, Massachusetts. Also known as the Babson Farm Quarry, it closed in 1929, eventually becoming a state park. The quarry is an impressive site, and its proximity to the ocean gives the visitor a unique opportunity to see nature's work, as well. Rambling through the heath you may come across massive granite stones cut from the quarry walls, or cut stones smoothed over time by the actions of the sea. The only thing I don't recommend is swimming; the quarry is off-limits for this activity, as the currents in the ocean are strong.

Odiorne Point State Park—Rye, NH, and Pemaquid Point Light—Bristol, ME

Prolific stone-stacking sites.

Ogunquit Beach—Ogunquit, ME

Gold

The Beach at Ogunquit, Maine, and the Josias River that feeds it, was once the site of gold rush fever. In 1960, while dredging Perkins Cove, the project engineer found traces of gold in the gravel dumped in the municipal parking lot. This discovery started a rush of "prospectors" into town, from around New England and beyond. Newspapers reported nearly 2,500 adventurers chasing their dreams in the town beach's municipal parking lot. Most were tight-lipped about their success or failure, leaving some to believe there wasn't any gold to begin with, but you never know. So for the curious reading this, you might want to grab your pie plates and head to Ogunquit; it could make for an interesting day.

Little Hunters Beach—Acadia National Park, ME

Little Hunters Beach is just down the road from Sand Beach. Secluded and usually missed by tourists, it's a great place to sit and meditate. The water washing back through the stones is relaxing and almost Zen-like. The beach is a tapestry of red, black, gray, orange, and pink granite stones secluded between two headlands.

Monument Cove—Acadia National Park, ME

Monument Beach is just beyond Thunder Hole on the Park Loop Trail. The pink granite cliffs are eroding, giving the impression at times that someone may have stacked up the stones here. On the contrary, these are natural formations, contrasting sharply with the beach boulders that have been rounded by years of rolling in the sea. This is a very special place.

Quoddy Head—Lubec, ME

Maine has some of the prettiest cobbled beaches in New England, and Quoddy Head, located on Maine's Bold Coast, has some of the best. Visit the beach just below Quoddy Head Light; there are stairs, or you can take the trail just south for some spectacular views.

Shipwrecks

My fascination with shipwrecks might have something to do with my experience owning boats. My first boat was an old lapstrake that became a shipwreck the day it was launched, and every day thereafter at high tide. I should have known: Paint is no substitute for clench nails. My second boat went down during a hurricane, and I learned more than I ever wanted to know about maritime law and obstructions to navigation in harbors.

—Author

The shores of New England have always been a dangerous place, more ships having been lost along this coastline than any other place in America. Massachusetts's Cape Cod is particularly treacherous, with swift ocean currents, changing shoal water, and strong longshore drift. The stretch of sand from Chatham to Provincetown alone is home to more than three thousand wrecks.

Two of the more famous ships dashed along the outer Cape are the HMS *Somerset*, a British man-of-war that sailed these waters during the American Revolution, and "Black Sam" Bellamy's pirate ship, the *Whydah*. The *Somerset* is exposed infrequently these days, but one good storm is all it takes to drag enough sand off the beach to reveal her remains. The *Somerset* was a British ship of the line and spent time blockading Boston Harbor when it wasn't chasing French privateers who were attempting to aid the colonies during their War of Independence. It was during one of these chases that the *Somerset* grounded at Peaked Hill Bar, meeting its untimely end.

The *Whydah*, Samuel Bellamy's pirate ship, became stranded on a bar during a nor'easter, taking the captain, crew, and treasure to the bottom. Bellamy was attempting to sail around the tip of the Cape to reach the safer waters of Massachusetts Bay, but wrecked when he was lured onto one of the notorious Cape sandbars in the vicinity of today's Marconi Beach. The location of the wreck and the size of its treasure was only a matter of speculation until modern-day treasure hunter Barry Clifford located it in 1984.

There are many reasons why ships wreck. In the early days of America, ships were the transportation of choice for most goods and materials, and thousands of ships plied the waters of the Atlantic, moving goods and raw material from one place to another. Weather forecasting was primitive, navigation was an art, charts were often inaccurate or nonexistent, and the main source of power was the wind. Other reasons for New England's large watery graveyard include war, bad ship design, lousy captaining, and simple abandonment of boats and ships once they'd outlived their usefulness. Like farmers leaving obsolete equipment sitting at the edge of a field, many early mariners drove their unserviceable ships and boats up a creek or onto the shore to be burned or consumed by time and the elements.

Rhode Island has almost two thousand shipwrecks in its coastal waters, including a very interesting ships' graveyard in Newport Harbor. The British sank thirteen of their own ships there to keep the French from sailing in and attacking their positions during the Revolutionary War. Most were transports placed in service to bring the British Army to America. They were large bulky vessels of little consequence, with one notable exception: Captain James Cook's bark, the *Endeavour*. Cook was a captain in the British Navy who, during his three expeditions of discovery, mapped more of the oceans and continents of the globe than any other person in naval history. The *Endeavour* was the ship Captain Cook sailed when he first circumnavigated the world.

As beachcombers we'll never run into the *Endeavour* or the *Whydah* as we explore New England's beaches and strands, but other ships are there for the viewing, some with interesting stories of their own, and others, still shrouded in mystery. Here's a few that you can try to find as you start your exploration.

OYSTER BOAT WRECK–WELLFLEET, MA

Most people who drove through Wiscasset, Maine, during the last two thirds of the twentieth century will remember the two four-masted schooners *Hesper* and *Luther Little*, tied up and abandoned at the dock. They defined the Maine coast for many visitors and added to the nostalgic view of what it meant to vacation along the coast. They've been gone now for almost fifteen years, unceremoniously hauled to a landfill, but their memory lives on.

On a much smaller scale and with little fanfare is the deteriorating hulk of the Wellfleet oyster boat sitting in Duck Creek on Cape Cod. Her back is broken and she's rotting away as she succumbs to the elements, but in many

ways, I'm as intrigued by this old pile of wooden bones as I was with the *Hesper* and her mate.

For many years Wellfleet defined oystering in Massachusetts, and Duck Creek was its epicenter. When the railroad arrived in 1870, cutting access to the creek, most boats moved outside, and the creek entered a new phase in its life as a quiet backwater conservation area. Not all the boats moved, however; some stayed, and in the balance of nature, a colony of native oysters looking for a place to put a foot down, attached themselves to this wreck. As this old wooden boat slowly dissolves into the creek, the shellfish it once so avidly harvested now call this wreck their home.

To visit the site, you should cross over "Tim's Bridge" to the Cannon Hill conservation area and follow the trail around to the remains of the old railroad bridge. Just around the corner to the left of the bridge, and visitable at low tide, is the wreck.

MISERY ISLAND WRECK: *CITY OF ROCKLAND*–BEVERLY HARBOR, MA

On July 26, 1904, while cruising in dense fog, the 274-foot steamship *City of Rockland* grounded on Gangway Ledge in Penobscot Bay. She was eventually towed to Boston for repairs, and it's at this point the story gets a little fuzzy. Photographs from the Libby Collection in the Boston Public Library show the steamer under repair in 1913. It also shows pictures of the steamer sunk at the pier in Boston. Whatever the timing of events, the ship was eventually placed out of service and stripped of anything valuable. While being towed north, she ended up between Little Misery and Great Misery Islands in Beverly Harbor, Massachusetts, where she burned. Some say vandals fired the ship; others say the owner burned her to salvage anything else of value. One other twist to this story is my great-uncle's recollection. He was a sea captain out of Beverly, and remembered the ship catching fire while under tow and being grounded between the two islands, allowing it to burn out. Whatever the actual truth, today the remains of the *City of Rockland* sit in about eight feet of water protruding at low tide, her ribs covered in seaweed but still distinguishable after all these years.

COFFIN'S BEACH WRECK–GLOUCESTER, MA

On an early July morning, a shipwreck was discovered on Coffin's Beach in Gloucester, Massachusetts, and like many wrecks, most of the hull lies tantalizingly below the sand. Markings on the stem indicate that much of the

boat's remains are still buried at least six feet under the sand. She looks to be about forty feet in length, and her remains are being investigated by the Massachusetts Board of Underwater Archaeological Resources and Harold Burnham, a master shipwright from Essex, Massachusetts. Lying parallel to the beach, wave action and currents have buried much of her seaward side, but her landward side is more exposed, and planking can still be seen attached to her framing. No metal fastenings were discovered, and telltale round holes indicate she was trunnel (wooden dowel) fastened. Harold Burnham believes she could be a pinky, a common early design, and may date to the early colonial or Revolutionary War period, making her at least two hundred years old. The team was able to dig down far enough to inspect her ballast stones, some of which were coral in origin, indicating the ship had sailed at some point to the tropics. As with most wrecks, there are no plans to excavate the remains, and she will probably be left alone, eventually covered back over, allowing her to reappear at some future time to the surprise of another generation of beachgoers.

PINKY SCHOONER–ESSEX, MA

The shipwreck on Short Sands Beach has been identified by some as a pinky, or a pink. If it is a pinky, it was schooner-rigged, not square-rigged as some suggest. Pinks and pinkies are two-masted boats, the main difference being

that pinkies are schooner-rigged. Anyone who would like to see a traditional pinky hull should travel to Essex, Massachusetts, home of the Burnham Boatyard. The boatyard has been in the Burnham family for seven generations, and current owner Harold Burnham is the last of the traditional wooden boat builders of Essex. Harold recently built himself a new pinky, and after stripping his old boat of everything usable, he did what many old-timers used to do. He moved the old shell up into the creek where she sits today, slowly succumbing to the elements. If you do visit Essex, you should stop at the Essex Shipbuilding Museum, a great vantage point from which to view Harold's boatyard. You'll get a chance to see the tired old pinky *Maine* sitting in her final resting spot, as time and the elements do their work.

ADA K. DAMON–IPSWICH, MA

On December 25, 1909, a terrible storm raged along the Northeast coast, leaving many shipwrecks in its wake. One of those was the unlucky schooner *Ada K. Damon*. Built in Essex by Ebenezer Burnham in 1875, she found herself stranded on that fateful Christmas Day, high up in the sand on Steep Hill Beach. She measured eighty feet long and twenty-three feet wide and was built for fishing the Grand Banks, but by 1909 she'd been reduced to hauling sand for her new owner, Captain Brewster. He had recently sold his farm in

Maine and put all the proceeds into the *Ada K.* This was his first, and last, trip. He ended up back in Maine with shattered dreams and no money, looking for farm work. The *Ada K.* has stayed anchored to the beach ever since. She appears every few decades, and 2015 was her latest sighting.

SCHOONER *JENNIE M. CARTER*–SALISBURY BEACH, MA

The *Jennie Carter* was a 297-ton, 130-foot three-masted schooner built in Newton, Maryland, in 1874. During a violent storm in April of 1894 she suffered some damage, including the loss of her rudder. She was spotted floundering off Cape Cod's Highland Light on April 10, but her captain declined assistance. Three days later the ship was spotted again, this time drifting along the beach in Salisbury, nearly a hundred miles from her original position. The schooner eventually grounded on the beach not far from the present-day Sea Glass Restaurant.

When men from the Plum Island Lifesaving Station boarded the *Jennie*, they confirmed that the crew was gone, with the exception of the ship's cat. She was sitting in the captain's cabin keeping warm by the still-lit fire in the stove. It's speculated that the crew was probably washed overboard during the storm. The ship's cargo was granite blocks, and once she grounded it wasn't long before the keel snapped, breaking her back and making her a total loss. The granite was offloaded and sold at auction. The ship, being unsalvageable, has remained in the same spot where she grounded over 120 years ago.

Today, at low tide, she sits just below the surface, her ribs creating swirling motions on the surface of the sea, giving the impression that something big and ominous lies just out of sight. In the winter of 2013 the beach suffered considerable erosion, and the *Jennie M. Carter* rose back into view, an impressive spectacle, and a unique part of the history of Salisbury.

SHORT SANDS BEACH WRECK—YORK, ME

The mystery that surrounds the wreck at Short Sands Beach in York, Maine, is a tantalizing one. The hulk is hidden from view at the moment, but with each winter storm the chance of seeing her becomes a distinct possibility. She showed herself in 1958, and then in the 1960s, '70s, '80s, and '90s, and again most recently in 2013. She's a fifty-one-foot sloop that state archaeologists believe is from the Revolutionary War period, although others speculate she's a little younger than that. Her identity is still unknown, which is no surprise; ships went down all the time during the days of sail. York alone has at least sixty-seven shipwrecks, and less than a third of them have actually been located. I visited the site in 2014, and at low tide all I saw was sand. It was still a gratifying experience to know that just a few feet under the sand on the spot where I stood, history rested, to be resurrected at any time.

D. T. SHERIDAN–MONHEGAN ISLAND, ME

The *D. T. Sheridan* was a 110-foot steel-hulled diesel tugboat built in 1939 in Brooklyn, New York. In 1948, while towing barges in dense fog, the *Sheridan* ran aground and eventually ended up on the rocks at Lobster Cove, on the south side of Monhegan Island in Maine. The hull and various other sections of the boat are easily viewed because the boat sits on the rocks, completely out of the water, a testament to the power of the sea.

Monhegan Island is located ten miles off the Maine coast, and can be reached by ferry from the fishing village of Port Clyde. The Monhegan Boat Line leaves daily from the local wharf, ferrying people out on the mailboat *Elizabeth Ann*, or the sixty-five-foot *Laura B.*, the latter a historic World War II patrol boat formerly known as a US Army T-57. The *Laura B.* saw action in the Pacific Theater as both a patrol boat and troop carrier.

Sea Glass and Pottery Shards

The sea does not reward those who are too anxious, too greedy, or too impatient. One should lie empty, open, choiceless as a beach—waiting for a gift from the sea.

—*Anne Morrow Lindbergh*

One of the best places to find sea glass today is on Spectacle Island in Boston Harbor. The island has a storied past and served many purposes over the years, including as a Native American fishing camp and a horse-rendering plant, and lastly, as a city dump. Boston piled its rubbish on Spectacle until 1959, when the city decided it just couldn't stack rubbish any higher on this small harbor island. The island was an eyesore until 1992, when it was remediated as part of Boston's Big Dig project. It was capped with millions of cubic yards of fill, trees and ground cover were planted, and a beach was created. Today it's part of the Boston Harbor Islands National Park. Even with all the topsoil that was added, there's still a great deal of glass and pottery that somehow finds its way onto the beach. Maybe a lot of it fell off the rubbish pile and into the harbor before the island was reclaimed. Whatever the reason, there's always sea glass and pottery shards to be found, some very old, and almost all pre-1959. The only drawback for avid collectors is a restriction on taking any of the glass and shards off the island. The Massachusetts Department of Conservation and Recreation (DCR) wants the material to remain, to be enjoyed by future generations.

For sea glass that you *can* take home, almost any beach will yield a piece if you search long enough. For thousands of years, ocean dumping

was considered the cleanest and healthiest way to dispose of refuse, and local communities dumped anything and everything into the sea, believing in its unlimited ability to absorb waste. Landfills were dirty and smelly, attracting disease-carrying vermin that threatened the health and safety of local

populations. "Out of sight, out of mind" dumping in the ocean offered an instant solution to a very real health hazard. The ocean was also the superhighway of commerce for early America, and many cargos in the pre-plastic era met an untimely end when they went down with the ship. The most common source of sea glass, though, is probably from people throwing bottles into the ocean from land or off boats close to shore.

With the advent of recycling and the idea that a weathered piece of beach glass is a collectible item, glass once common on almost any beach has become a rarer find these days for most beachcombers.

The common sea glass colors today are lime green, brown, and clear (white). These are the colors of glass used for most soda, beer, and other beverage containers. Red and blue glass is rare, black glass is very rare, and orange glass is one of the rarest of colors. Black glass is often old and thick antique glass that required additives such as iron to improve its strength.

Well-tumbled sea glass usually looks frosted. This is caused by long exposure to salt water that over time, with constant tumbling, leaches out the soda and lime in the glass, creating this frosted effect.

SPECIAL PLACES

Sea glass is found on every beach in New England, but some are better for glass collecting than others. Because this prized collectible is actually a discarded man-made material, beaches near populous areas, especially older cities and towns, are some of the best places to find it. Many people make a distinction between *beach glass* (freshwater) and *sea glass* (salt water). We don't, but for the sake of discussion, we'll refer to the glass we discuss in this book as sea glass. As glass is discarded into the sea, tides and currents move these shards around, depositing many into bays and coves up-current. During storms when weather-related activities strip beaches of sand and other materials, sea glass can be redistributed to other areas. The smoother frosted glass is the most sought after, and usually is older than clear glass, but with sea glass becoming scarcer by the year, any glass—with the exception of newly deposited shards—is considered collectible.

We've always had good luck finding sea glass at these beaches:
- Fort Adams State Park, Newport, RI
- Winter Island, Salem, MA
- Lynch Park, Beverly, MA
- Plum Island, Newburyport, MA
- Salisbury Beach, Salisbury, MA
- Spring Point Beach, Portland, ME
- East End Beach, Portland, ME
- Laite Memorial Beach, Camden, ME

Pirate Treasure and Gold

> The spirit of true adventure lives in the soul of the treasure hunter. The odds may be a thousand to one that he will unearth a solitary doubloon, yet he is lured to undertake the most prodigious exertions by the keen zest of the game itself.
> —*Ralph D. Paine,* The Book of Buried Treasure

Pirates. Yes, pirates!

The Northeast coast has always offered a multitude of intriguing locations for maritime bandits to employ their particular skills. Many of the most infamous and legendary pirates that sailed during this Golden Age, men like William Kidd, "Black Sam" Bellamy, John Quelch, and Thomas Tew, sailed the New England shore. The New England shoreline is also a good place to hide treasure. Marblehead Harbor, the Isles of Shoals, Gloucester's Snake Island, Gardner's Island, Machiasport, Monhegan, and Pond Islands are all considered likely spots for pirate treasure.

The pirates who roamed the New England coast have been romanticized in American culture and maritime lore. Boldly dressed in an array of strange outfits, often concocted with items seized from captured ships, these buccaneers sailed this rugged coastline raiding and pillaging—and sometimes hiding and burying—everything they could get their hands on.

Today their stories may be more legend than fact, more fiction than truth, but the possibility, however slim, of buried treasure is an allure that for most of us is irresistible.

Some "pirates," like William Kidd, may not have been pirates at all. It wasn't difficult for an adventurous privateer, caught up in the politics and shady business dealing of the day, to find himself branded a pirate upon his return from sea. Privateers were only allowed to prey upon their nation's

enemies, and more than one honest privateer was branded a pirate for attacking and seizing the wrong ship. When Captain Kidd found out he'd been accused of piracy, he sailed from his home in New York to Boston in hopes of clearing his name. After all, he'd been commissioned by some of the most powerful men in England's government to prey on enemies of the British Crown, especially pirates. In effect, he was a pirate hunter working for his own government. Kidd was no fool, and knew the risk of trying to prove his innocence. We know that he stopped off at a number of islands and mainland coves on his trip to Boston, and it's been speculated that he buried much of his treasure in some of these places, to be used if necessary as a bargaining tool to buy his freedom. This speculation was strengthened when some of his treasure was discovered on Gardner's Island, off the east end of Long Island.

Many people believe that with a ship's hold full of treasure, and knowing he'd been accused of piracy, Kidd would have needed to find more than one spot to deposit his loot as he sailed to Boston to establish his innocence. Coburn's Island, Thirty Mile Island, Hammonasset Beach, Money Island (one of the Thimble Islands), and Charles Island (in Milford, part of Silver Sands State Park), are all places laced with folklore and speculation around Captain Kidd and his missing treasure. Of these, Charles Island is your best bet if you'd like to take a look around. The island today is a bird sanctuary and the former site of a Catholic retreat. While some structures still remain, the birds are definitely in charge of the property today.

Although Kidd and his crew were spotted on Charles Island by local citizens who chased after them, the island has a storied past, not only involving pirates. The island is said to be cursed—not once, not twice, but three times. A chief of the local Paugussett Indians cursed the island sometime after the tribe sold it to the Europeans. According to legend, it was cursed a second time by Captain Kidd, whose ghost is said to protect his treasure. And it was cursed a third time when a sailor buried treasure stolen from an Aztec king.

There's no official transportation to Charles Island, and it's recommended that anyone wishing to visit should use a boat, but if you're a true pirate lover, you can walk to the island while the tide is out. The island is accessible by a tombolo—a rocky bar that exposes itself at low tide. Pay close attention to the tides, though; it's dangerous to walk the tombolo, and if you choose this route and don't give yourself enough time, you'll be stranded until the bar reappears with the next low tide. More than one person has been pulled off this temporary bridge and drowned by the incoming rip.

Another location thought to hold Captain Kidd's treasure is Governor's Island in Boston Harbor. A letter supposedly written by Kidd during his incarceration in Boston, to his attorney in New York, was discovered in 1849 in Palmer, Massachusetts. At the time it was considered authentic, and that claim has never been refuted. Gallops Island in Boston Harbor is considered one of the islands that may hold Kidd's treasure, along with diamonds buried by pirate "Long Ben" Avery.

When I want to look for pirate treasure, I visit Cape Cod and spend time walking some part of Great Beach. Great Beach, as Thoreau called it, "is the beach of smooth and gently sloping sand, a dozen rods in width; with an endless series of white breakers, and light green water breaking over the bar, which runs the whole length of the forearm of the Cape." For Thoreau this was a very pretty sight, but the endless series of breakers and light green water over the bar have sent more ships to the bottom than almost any other strip of beach in America.

One of those was Captain Samuel Bellamy's pirate ship, the *Whydah*. Bellamy and his crew joined Davy Jones in his locker on April 26, 1717, when the *Whydah* grounded on a Cape Cod bar, broke up, and sank during a violent nor'easter. Upon hearing of the wreck, local inhabitants hurried to the site and, as was the custom in those days, scavenged and combed the shoreline for anything and everything they could use, leaving little behind for the governor's representative, Captain Cyprian Southark, when he arrived a few days later. Southark did manage to coerce some of the locals into returning what

they'd taken, but it wasn't much. The largest accumulation he ended up with for his troubles were the bodies of the dead pirates. The most important thing he accomplished in this misguided attempt to recover treasure for the governor of Massachusetts was the map he created of the wreck site. It became a real-life treasure map 274 years later when Barry Clifford used it to assist him in discovering the wreck. Clifford has recovered thousands of items, including gold coins, silver, weapons, and the ship's bell.

Marblehead and Gloucester, Massachusetts, and New Hampshire's Isles of Shoals are places of interest for anyone searching for John Quelch's pirate treasure. This well-documented story begins in Marblehead, where Quelch and others commandeered a brigantine named the *Charles* after throwing its sick captain overboard in Massachusetts Bay. From July 1703 until May 1704, Quelch and crew attacked and looted ships in the South Atlantic, amassing a large treasure, including a great amount of gold dust and silver ingots.

The pirates eventually returned to Marblehead, trying to pass

themselves off as privateers, but it didn't take long for the true story to emerge, once alcohol had loosened crew members' tongues. Some of the crew was quickly rounded up, including Captain Quelch, but many escaped and headed for the Isles of Shoals after brief stops in Salem and Gloucester. It's speculated that some of the treasure was hidden in Gloucester, most likely in the vicinity of Snake Island, but the largest amount of ill-gotten gains is most likely buried at the Isles of Shoals, where many of the pirates were actually caught in the act of burying some of the treasure. Only sixty-five pounds of gold dust was recovered, and not a sign of the gems or more than two hundred bars of silver was ever found. It's a good bet even today that Captain Quelch's treasure is still hidden, either in close proximity to Marblehead Harbor, on Snake Island off Gloucester, or on Smuttynose, Star, or Appledore Islands at the Isles of Shoals.

The Isles of Shoals may also hold other pirate treasure. Edward Teach, better known as Blackbeard, was one of the most notorious pirates ever to roam the Atlantic Ocean, and he spent considerable time living on Star Island.

Island historians can't agree on where Teach's treasure is hidden, but one thing they do agree on: It's hidden someplace on the Isles of Shoals. For his part, Blackbeard was quoted as saying, "Nobody but the devil and myself knows where my treasure is."

Ned Low buried some of his treasure, including silver bars, a chest of gold, and jewels, at the Isles of Shoals, most likely on either Smuttynose or Duck Island, and some believe on Pond Island in Maine's Casco Bay. The story of Pond Island is that Ned rowed to the island with two other pirates and buried the treasure—and the other pirates—in a marshy area near a pond. He never got the chance to retrieve it. Shortly thereafter, fed up with his psychopathic behavior, his crew set him adrift to die.

One of the stranger stories probably holding some grain of truth is the story of a pirate "settlement" started at Machiasport, Maine. The story about this haven for pirates centers around Black Sam Bellamy and Paulsgrave Williams, who were supposed to have built a fort complete with defensive positions and earthworks in the vicinity of Rocky Renshaw Point and the Old River Bridge. It's also rumored they built a vault some distance from the fort, in which to store their treasure.

One thing we do know: The locals have been running around for years looking for the treasure site, but to date have come up empty.

Beaches

CONNECTICUT
Great Captain Island

Greenwich, CT

Great Captain Island is the largest of three islands. The town operates a ferry service to the island, from the landing at Roger Sherman Baldwin Park, from mid-June to mid-September. Parking is available across Arch Street. There are trails, picnic tables, grills, restrooms, and posted swimming areas. Lifeguards are on duty from Memorial Day weekend through Labor Day weekend from 10 a.m. to 6 p.m. Leashed dogs are allowed into the park from December 1 through March 31.

Fees: Park/beach passes are required from May 1 to October 31.

Island Beach

Greenwich, CT

Island Beach, formerly known as Little Captain Island, is located about two miles south of Greenwich Harbor. During the summer months, the town-operated ferry service from Roger Sherman Baldwin Park shuttles beachgoers to this little gem. Just as with Great Captain Island, parking is available across Arch Street. Lifeguards are on duty from Memorial Day weekend through Labor Day weekend from 10 a.m. to 6 p.m. Leashed dogs are allowed in the park from December 1 through March 31.

Fees: Park/beach passes are required from May 1 to October 31.

Greenwich Point

Old Greenwich, CT

The beach and park at Greenwich Point are open daily from 6 a.m. until sunset. This is a great place to swim, hike, and explore. Other activities include picnicking, sailboarding, and fishing. As at other parks in the area, leashed dogs are allowed in the park from December 1 through March 31. Lifeguards are on duty from Memorial Day weekend through Labor Day weekend from 10 a.m. to 6 p.m.

Fees: Park/beach passes are required from May 1 to October 31.

Cove Island Park

Cove Road, Stamford, CT

Cove Island Park has a sandy beach, although sometimes cobbled, that faces Long Island Sound and is adjacent to tidal wetlands. The park is also home to Quigley Beach, a small section of coved beach with a jetty that can be used for fishing. Cove Island Park sits just across the water from Weed Beach. Amenities include a pier for fishing, picnic area, nature center, concession stands, and restrooms. This beach/park is a great place to go for a swim, for fishing or crabbing, or bird watching. Lifeguards are on duty during the summer season, Memorial Day to Labor Day, and much of the park is wheelchair-accessible.

Fees: Nonresident daily and seasonal passes to the park can be purchased at the park gate, or at the cashier's office in the Stamford Government Center building at 888 Washington Boulevard, Stamford.

Weed Beach

Nearwater Lane, Darien, CT

Weed Beach is another typical Connecticut beach with a bathhouse, tennis courts, fitness trail, concession stands, and play area. Most of the beach is sandy. It's well protected, and wave action is usually mild. Lifeguards are on duty during the summer season, from Memorial Day to mid-September.

Fees: Parking fee.

Pear Tree Point Beach

Pear Tree Point Road, Darien, CT

Pear Tree Point Beach encompasses eight acres of land at the mouth of the Goodwives River in Darien. The sand is coarse but the beach is usually free of seaweed, and the water is a tad warmer than that of most ocean beaches in the Northeast. Its protected location helps keep the wave action to a minimum, but there is a crosscurrent at times because of its location. It has a large parking area and offers food concessions, boat launching, a picnic area, and restroom facilities. Lifeguards are on duty during the summer months.

Fees: Parking fee.

Calf Pasture Beach

Calf Pasture Beach Road, Norwalk, CT

Calf Pasture Beach is part of a thirty-three-acre beach/park. There is a fishing area, softball fields, skateboard park, volleyball courts, sailboat and windsurf rentals, and more. Lifeguards are on duty during the summer season, June to September. Food is available at Ripka's Beach Café and at the courtyard by Calfé Mu. Pets are not allowed.

Fees: Day parking passes. Passes can be downloaded at the Norwalk Park and Recreation site online, and are also available at the beach.

Compo Beach

60 Compo Beach Road, Westport, CT

Compo Beach is part of a twenty-nine-acre park on Long Island Sound. It's a large sandy beach bordering the Saugatuck River. It is wheelchair-accessible, with restroom facilities, boardwalk, pavilion, concession stand, and lockers. Lifeguards are on duty during the summer season, Memorial Day to Labor Day, 10 a.m. to 6 p.m. The beach is open year-round, and dog-friendly from October 1 through March 30 in designated off-leash areas. Open 4 a.m. to 10 p.m.

Fees: A daily fee is charged to park from May 1 through September 30.

Burying Hill Beach

Burying Hill Road and Beachside Avenue, Westport, CT

Burying Hill Beach is a sand and rock beach along the shore of Long Island Sound. It has restroom and changing facilities, and an area for cookouts that includes picnic tables and grills. The park is open May 1 through September 30 from 5 a.m. to 10 p.m. Lifeguards are on duty from Memorial Day to Labor Day, 10 a.m. to 6 p.m. Dog-friendly from October 1 through March 31.

Fees: Motor vehicles and motorcycles may enter the beach with a valid Parks and Recreation parking sticker, or by paying the daily fee. Parking fees are required from Memorial Day to October 1.

Penfield Beach

323 Fairfield Beach Road, Fairfield, CT

Penfield Beach is a long, sandy beach, and a typical Connecticut beach complex with concession stands, banquet facilities, rentable lockers, picnic tables, and restroom facilities. The beach is wheelchair-accessible and free to the public. Lifeguards are on duty during the summer season, Memorial Day to Labor Day.

Fees: During the summer season a parking sticker is required to park in the lot. Vehicles without a sticker may pay a daily fee.

Jennings Beach

880 South Benson Road, Fairfield, CT

This is a large sandy beach located next to a boat marina. It has a concession stand and restroom facilities. The beach is free and open to the public, but there is a parking fee during the summer season. Lifeguards are on duty during the summer season from mid-June to Labor Day. The beach is open to dogs and horses from October 1 to March 31.

Fees: Parking fee during the summer season.

Saint Mary's by the Sea

Eames Boulevard (via Gilman Street), Bridgeport, CT

Outdoor enthusiasts will love Saint Mary's by the Sea, located in the Black Rock neighborhood of Bridgeport. This beach is a great place for bird- and wildlife watching. There is a half-mile walkway for strolling, which provides visitors with spectacular views of Long Island Sound and Black Rock Harbor. Parts of the park are wheelchair-accessible.

Fees: Parking fee; contact the Bridgeport Parks and Recreation Department to obtain a parking permit to visit this site. There is also on-street parking.

Seaside Park Beach

Barnum Dyke, Bridgeport, CT

Designed by Calvert Vaux and Frederick Law Olmsted, Seaside Park Beach features 325 acres of lawns, glades, and sports fields on Long Island Sound, offering the visitor more than three miles of beautiful sandy coastline for sunning, swimming, or strolling. Fayerweather Island, a natural wildlife preserve, is at the western end of the park, accessed by crossing the breakwater. Amenities include a picnic area, concession stands, bathhouse, and restrooms. Lifeguards are on duty during the summer season, Memorial Day to Labor Day.

Fees: Park fees are required if entering by car.

Long Beach

Oak Bluff, Stratford, CT

Long Beach is located between Long Island Sound and the Great Meadows tidal marsh. It is a barrier beach with sand dunes, and at times is home to nesting piping plovers. This makes the beach and surrounding area a great place for bird watching. Fishing is allowed outside of designated swimming areas (the eastern end of the beach is one such area). You'll need to bring your own snacks, as Long Beach is considered an "unimproved" beach, and has no food concessions or permanent restroom facilities.

Fees: A parking permit is required from May 31 until Labor Day.

Short Beach

1 Dorne Drive, Stratford, CT

Short Beach is located adjacent to the mouth of the Housatonic River and a great fishing spot, especially for striped bass and bluefish. Amenities include a picnic area, playground, concession stand, showers, and restroom facilities. Some sections of the beach are wheelchair-accessible. Part of the beach is cordoned off because it's a designated piping plover nesting area during part of the summer season. Parking is available, and lifeguards are on duty during the summer season, June to September.

Walnut Beach

Park Avenue and East Broadway, Milford, CT

Walnut Beach is a large sandy beach and a great place to spend the day strolling along the edge of Long Island Sound or fishing from the pier. Amenities include a pier, concession stands, picnic area, supervised swimming area, restrooms, fishing, and shell fishing. Lifeguards are on duty during the summer season, Memorial Day through Labor Day weekend (July 1 to August 17 daily, otherwise weekends only). This is a great location for shell collecting, as well as fishing from the breakwater and crabbing from shore.

Fees: There is a daily or seasonal admission fee, but the site provides ample parking. Nonresidents visiting Walnut Beach must park in the rear of the main parking lot.

Silver Sands State Park

Silver Sands Park Road, Milford, CT

Silver Sands is a large sandy beach and home to Charles Island, the popular (presumed) site of Captain Kidd's buried treasure. The island is connected to the mainland by a sand/gravel bar also known as a tombolo, submerged at high tide. Captain Kidd is reputed to have buried his treasure on the island in 1699. The island also contains the remains of a Catholic retreat center from the 1930s. Activities include swimming, fishing, boating, crabbing, and treasure hunting. There's a boardwalk connecting Silver Sands with Milford's Walnut Beach Park, and restroom facilities are available at both beaches. Lifeguards are on duty in posted, supervised swimming areas during the summer season, Memorial Day through Labor Day. For those wishing to reach Charles Island, accessing the tombolo is extremely dangerous and should not be attempted. Access to the island is prohibited May 1 through August 31 to protect heron and egret rookeries. Access to the park in the evening is available to marine anglers only via the small parking area at the end of East Broadway, located at the south-central end of the park.

Fees: The park includes a large parking area, and admission to the park is free.

Gulf Beach

Gulf Street, Milford, CT

Gulf Beach is a sandy beach fronting Long Island Sound and a good location for swimming and bird watching. Parts of the site, including a fishing pier, are wheelchair-accessible. Amenities include a picnic area, concession stand, and restrooms. The beach is fronted by Charles Island, rumored to be the location of pirate Captain Kidd's treasure. There is on-site parking at the park, for residents, and on-site nonresident parking located across the street. Lifeguards are on duty during the summer season, Memorial Day through Labor Day weekend (July 1 to August 17 daily, otherwise weekends only).

Fees: Variable parking fees for residents and nonresidents.

Morse Beach

Morse Avenue / Beach Street, West Haven, CT

Morse Beach is part of West Haven's three-and-a-half-mile urban greenway waterfront park. It's a large sandy beach with good locations for swimming and fishing, with amenities including restroom facilities, food concessions, picnic area, and wildlife viewing. The beach is open from 9 a.m. until sunset, and lifeguards are on duty during the summer season, Memorial Day through Labor Day weekend.

Fees: Variable fee admission and daily parking fees for nonresidents from Memorial Day to Labor Day.

Bradley Point Beach

Savin Rock Trail, West Haven, CT

Bradley Point Beach is part of an interconnected waterfront urban greenway from Bradley Point Park to Sandy Point. There are few amenities, and the restroom facilities are portable toilets. The beach has a parking lot, although it's small. Lifeguards are on duty during the summer season, Memorial Day through Labor Day weekend.

Lighthouse Point Park

Lighthouse Road, New Haven, CT

Lighthouse Point is located at the eastern point of New Haven Harbor in East Haven. Amenities include swimming, fishing, boating, picnicking, concession stand, and lighthouse tours. It is a popular spot for observing the monarch butterfly migration in the fall, and for bird watching, because of its location on the Atlantic flyway. The park is also home to The Carousel at Lighthouse Point Park, a historic facility housing an antique carousel. This historic building is available for private functions. The park is open daily from 7 a.m. until sunset, and lifeguards are on duty during the summer season, June to September.

Stony Creek Beach

Thimble Island Road, Branford, CT

The beach is located in the southeast section of Branford and open to the public. It is close to the town dock and pier, providing fishing opportunities. Close by is a small pocket beach. Both beaches have seating areas and limited short-term parking. There is also a drop-off area. The dock and pier are wheelchair-accessible. This beach is staffed with lifeguards from Memorial Day through Labor Day.

Hammonasset Beach State Park

1288 Boston Post Road, Madison, CT

Hammonasset Beach State Park has more than two miles of sandy beachfront and is Connecticut's largest shoreline park. The park is a prime location for observing the monarch butterfly migration, and has many other amenities, including swimming, camping, picnicking, saltwater fishing, biking, hiking, and boating. The beach and park are wheelchair-accessible. Concession stands and a boardwalk are located on-site, as well as a nature center with interpretive programs. Lifeguards are on duty during the summer season, Memorial Day through Labor Day. The beach is open from 8 a.m. until sunset, but campers and anglers with passes may enter the park during the evening hours.

Fees: Variable rate entrance fees depending on resident status and season.

Clinton Town Beach

Waterside Lane, Clinton, CT

This beach is adjacent to the Hammock River on Long Island Sound and is an ideal place for fishing. There are also tidal marshes that offer bird watching and other wildlife-viewing opportunities. The beach has access for car-top boat launchings, and amenities include restrooms, concession stands, and a covered picnic area. Lifeguards are on duty during the summer season, Memorial Day through Labor Day. Parking is available.

Fees: Entrance fee for residents and parking passes for nonresidents during the summer season.

Harvey's Beach

Route 154, Old Saybrook, CT

Harvey's Beach is a small, town-owned sandy beach with restrooms, bathhouse, showers, a concession stand, and a playground. The beach is open—and lifeguards are on duty—for the summer season, Memorial Day to Labor Day.

Fees: Entrance fee.

Sound View Beach

Hartford Avenue, Old Lyme, CT

This is a small, town-owned beach open to the public, but with limited parking and few amenities. There are no lifeguards on duty, so swimming is at your own risk. The beach is open from sunrise to sunset.

Rocky Neck State Park

Route 156, East Lyme, CT

Rocky Neck State Park is a wide sand beach and home to a large stone pavilion. Amenities include family camping at wooded and open campsites, saltwater fishing from the beach and stone jetty, and a wheelchair-accessible fishing pier. The park is a great place for those interested in bird watching, hiking, picnicking, fishing, crabbing, and swimming. Lifeguards are on duty during the summer season, Memorial Day through Labor Day. Open daily from 8 a.m. to sunset.

Fees: Variable parking fees apply between April and late September. There is also a camping fee for those who stay at the park.

Ocean Beach Park

1225 Ocean Avenue, New London, CT

Located on Ocean Avenue in New London is Ocean Beach Park, a large recreational facility. Amenities include a half-mile-long boardwalk, fifty-meter Olympic swimming pool, eighteen-hole miniature golf course, video arcade, and much more. If you're looking for a quiet beach to walk along the shore, this is not the one. Lifeguards are on duty during the summer season, Memorial Day to Labor Day, at the ocean and the pool.

DuBois Beach

Stonington, CT

DuBois Beach is located in the seaside village of Stonington. This sandy beach is family-oriented, with a pavilion and restroom facilities. The beach's 265 feet of shoreline fills up quickly, so plan to arrive early. Lifeguards are on duty during the summer season, June to September. Parking is available at the Stonington Point parking lot at the end of Water Street.

Fees: A day-use permit for the beach can be obtained on-site.

RHODE ISLAND
Watch Hill Beach (Carousel Beach)

151 Bay Street, Westerly, RI

This clean, serene beach in Westerly, Rhode Island, is located near an antique carousel. This is a family beach with small waves and a negligible undertow, located near the start of a one-mile walk to scenic Napatree Point. If you decide to hike the beach to Napatree Point, be sure to visit the now-defunct Fort Mansfield. It was built in 1898 as part of a coastal defense system. The Watch Hill Beach parking lot fills up early and street parking is very hard to find, so if you're visiting during the summer season, Memorial Day to Labor Day, get there early. Amenities include a bathhouse, restrooms, picnic area, snack bar, and wheelchair access. Lifeguards are on duty during the summer season.

Fees: Nominal parking fee.

Misquamicut State Beach

257 Atlantic Avenue, Westerly, RI

Misquamicut is a long, sandy state-run beach with over seven miles of shore-front. The beach is situated along Westerly's Atlantic Avenue. This is Rhode Island's largest beach and has beautiful clear-blue water with moderate surf, but beware of the small occasional undertow. Amenities include a picnic area, restrooms, showers, snack bar, pavilion, a large parking area, and an observation tower. This beach is a popular spot for board- and bodysurfing. Lifeguards are on duty daily during the summer season, Memorial Day to Labor Day.
Fees: Free beach entry, but variable parking fees.

Atlantic Beach Park

321 Atlantic Avenue, Westerly, RI

Rhode Island's Atlantic Beach Park is a family-oriented beach and offers plenty of opportunity for fun and recreation. Amenities include amusement rides, seafood restaurants, snack bars, waterslide, carousel, batting cages, game room, oceanside patio bar, and restrooms. Parts of the park are wheelchair-accessible. This park is more like an amusement park that just happens to be located at the seashore, so if you're looking for a quiet place to sit and relax, this is probably not the beach for you.
Fees: Parking fee from 8:00 a.m. to 4:30 p.m.

Wuskenau Town Beach

311 Atlantic Avenue, Westerly, RI

The Wuskenau Beach is a town-owned and -operated beach facility located next to Misquamicut State Beach. The facility is open to the public, and the summer season extends from Memorial Day through Labor Day, during which lifeguards are on duty. Amenities include restrooms, showers, chair/umbrella rentals, snack bar, lockers, bike racks, and complete wheelchair access. There are three acres of public beach to visit, just steps away from Atlantic Beach Park and concession stands.
Fees: Season passes are available to anyone regardless of residency. Day passes can be purchased on-site after Memorial Day weekend.

Blue Shutters Town Beach

469 East Beach Road, Charlestown, RI

Blue Shutters is a town-operated beach with moderate surf, fine sand, and a great view of Block Island Sound. It's also one of the better beaches in the area for shell collecting. Amenities include a snack bar, shower stations, picnic area, restrooms, and changing rooms. The beach also offers wheelchairs. This beach accepts resident and nonresident beach stickers, with a senior citizen discount available. Lifeguards are on duty during the summer season, Memorial Day to Labor Day.

Fees: Variable fees for parking.

East Beach / Ninigret Conservation Area

East Beach Road, Charlestown, RI

East Beach is a treasure. It's a spectacular barrier beach consisting of three miles of prime coastline at the eastern end of Quonochontaug Neck, one of the least-developed sections of shoreline in Rhode Island. East State Beach is a surf beach with limited parking. A small portion of the beach is staffed with lifeguards during the summer season, Memorial Day to Labor Day.

Fees: Vehicles driving on the barrier beach, as well as camping vehicles, require barrier beach passes. The beach offers a good opportunity for shell fishing, but a license is required for nonresidents. No pets allowed.

Charlestown Breachway State Beach

Charlestown Beach Road, Charlestown, RI

This sandy ocean beach popular with fishermen and windsurfers is located next to the Charlestown Breachway—a man-made channel in Charlestown, Rhode Island. Amenities include a swimming area, wheelchair accessibility, fishing pier, campsites, boat ramp, and restrooms. It's the only beach in the area that allows camping. Shell fishing is also allowed with the proper license, and there's parking for about a hundred cars. Lifeguards are on duty during the summer season, Memorial Day to Labor Day. The beach is open from dawn to dusk. Pets are not allowed on this beach.

Fees: Free beach entry, but variable parking fees.

Charlestown Town Beach

557 Charlestown Beach Road, Charlestown, RI

This town-operated saltwater beach has fine sand and moderate to heavy surf, with an occasional undertow. The beach is located adjacent to Charlestown Breachway State Beach. Amenities include picnic sites, restrooms, concession stands, and wheelchair access. No pets are allowed on the beach. Lifeguards are on duty during the summer season, Memorial Day to Labor Day.

Fees: Beach is free, but there are parking fees, variable depending on the day.

Baby Beach

Off Corn Neck Road near Dodge and Water Streets, New Shoreham (Block Island), RI

Known locally as Baby Beach, this section of coastline is located between Fred Benson Town Beach and Crescent Beach, beginning at the Surf Hotel on Corn Neck Road. This is where the locals take their children for a dip in the ocean. Calm waters and shallow tide pools make this a popular place for kids. Amenities include restrooms, showers, chair and umbrella rentals, snack bar, lockers, boogie board rentals, bike racks, and complete wheelchair access. There are no lifeguards on duty.

Fees: Admission and parking are free.

Ballard's Beach

End of Water Street, New Shoreham (Block Island), RI

Just south of the Block Island ferry dock and jetty is Ballard's Beach. This pet-friendly beach is busy and sometimes noisy because of its proximity to local restaurants. This is one of only two Block Island beaches with a lifeguard on duty. Amenities include restrooms, volleyball nets, picnic site, and chair/umbrella rentals.

Fees: Admission and parking are free.

Beach below Mohegan Bluffs

Off Spring Street / Mohegan Trail, New Shoreham (Block Island), RI

This is a beautiful and tranquil area with magnificent views and stunning landscapes. Parking is a short distance south of the lighthouse. The bluffs rise about two hundred feet above the sea and stretch for nearly three miles. There are stairs to the beach. This location offers spectacular vistas and nature walks. The summer season is from May 30 until Labor Day. There are few amenities, and no lifeguards on duty.

Fees: Admission is free.

Charleston Beach

End of Champlin Road, New Shoreham (Block Island), RI

This beach extends from Coast Guard Road to Block Island Sound and is a popular fishing location. The coarse sand beach is not crowded, and has no amenities. Parking is available at the end of Champlin Road, but because it's limited, the best transportation is by bike or on foot.

Fees: Admission is free.

Crescent Beach

Fred Benson Town Beach, 7 Corn Neck Road, New Shoreham (Block Island), RI

This two-mile-long beach located near the ferry dock is known locally as Crescent Beach. It is a popular spot for families because it's one of the few beaches on Block Island with lifeguards during the summer season, Memorial Day to Labor Day, and public amenities, which include a picnic site, chair and umbrella rentals, bike racks, free parking, wheelchair-accessible restrooms, showers, and a snack bar.

Fees: Admission is free.

Mansion Beach

Mansion Road, New Shoreham (Block Island), RI

Mansion Beach is marked by the stone foundation of Rhode Island's old Searles Mansion and dance hall. You can get to the beach by walking or biking along the road from Corn Neck. There is also a large parking lot, although the walk from the lot to the beach is a bit long. There are no amenities or lifeguards on duty here, but this is a popular beach for families nonetheless, and a good place for swimming and bodysurfing.

Fees: Free admission and parking.

Buttonwoods Beach / Warwick City Park

Warwick, RI

Buttonwoods Beach is a secluded sandy beach located in historic Warwick City Park. The beach is family-friendly, surrounded by walking trails, and easy to access. The waves are generally calm. This park has excellent accommodations for those using wheelchairs, bikes, and strollers, with benches and a boardwalk extending the length of the beach along Brush Neck Cove. Amenities include a playground, bicycle trails, dog park, picnic sites, shelters, restrooms, and snack bar. Lifeguards are on duty during the summer season, Memorial Day to Labor Day.

Fees: Admission fee in summer.

Conimicut Point Beach

Point Avenue, Warwick, RI

The beach is a sandy spit jutting out into Narragansett Bay, and a great spot for fishing, as well as catching some sun and swimming. Amenities include parking, a ramp for wheelchair access, restrooms, and a grassy picnic area.

Fees: Entrance fee.

Goddard Memorial State Park

345 Ives Road, Warwick, RI

This bayside park is great for walking, picnics, games, swimming, and horseback riding. Amenities include a boat-launching ramp, eighteen miles of bridle trails, a golf course, restrooms, and a picnic area. This is a nice spot for beachcombing, with shells and a chance to find sea glass. Some areas of the park are wheelchair-accessible. Lifeguards are on duty during the summer season, Memorial Day to Labor Day.

Fees: Parking fee.

Oakland Beach

Oakland Beach Avenue, Warwick, RI

Oakland Beach is a wide, sandy beach with a number of breakwaters. It extends nine hundred feet along the shore and is a relaxing place to take a swim. It offers an easily walkable shoreline, and is also a great place to fish or sunbathe. Amenities include a picnic site, wheelchair-accessible dock, a boat ramp, ball field, snack bar, and restrooms. Lifeguards are on duty during the summer season, June to September. If you do visit this beach, make sure to visit Iggy's Doughboys & Chowder House for their famous clam cakes, or try the St. Michelle Beach Club or Top of the Bay, just across the street.

Head's Beach (Jamestown Shores Beach)

Seaside Drive, Jamestown, RI

This tiny town beach has lots of seashells and rocks and not much sand, so bring shoes. While it's great for beachcombing and sunset walks, there is no lifeguard on duty. Parking is on a first-come, first-served basis. The beach is open from dawn to dusk.

Fees: Parking fees during the summer season (mid-June to September).

Bristol Town Beach

50 Asylum Road, Bristol, RI

This gravel beach is open for swimming, and lifeguards are on duty during the summer season, May through October. It's a great place to collect shells and has a number of amenities, including a picnic area and playground, as well as ample parking.

Fees: Parking fee during the summer season.

East Matunuck State Beach

950 Succotash Road, South Kingstown, RI

East Matunuck State Beach is located in a scenic marshland. This smaller and less-frequented white-sand beach is known for its vigorous waves and strong currents, making it an ideal spot for surfing. This is a great place to collect shells and to observe sea life such as starfish, crabs, and shellfish around the rocky reef that extends to the right of the beach. It has ample amenities, including a large parking lot, picnic areas, a jetty for fishing, restrooms and changing rooms, showers and lockers, a pavilion, and a snack bar. This beach has wheelchair access, and most areas are wheelchair-accessible. Lifeguards are on duty during the summer season, Memorial Day to Labor Day. No pets are allowed on the beach.

Fees: Free beach entry, but variable parking fees.

South Kingstown Town Beach at Matunuck

Matunuck Beach Road, South Kingstown, RI

This unprotected beach is located to the east of East Matunuck State Beach. The ocean often exhibits a rough surf and occasional riptides at this beach, and swimming is only recommended for strong swimmers. This beach is a great place for body- and board surfing for those who can handle the rough surf. Sunbathing is more the rule. Amenities include restrooms, changing rooms, wheelchair access, playground, volleyball court, picnic site, concessions, and a boardwalk. Lifeguards are on duty daily during the summer season, Memorial Day to Labor Day.

Fees: Variable-rate parking fees based on residency.

North Kingstown Town Beach

Beach Street, North Kingstown, RI

This small, town-operated beach offers a good amount of shade for those who need to stay out of the sun, and includes a grassy area for lounging. It's a great place to observe ocean creatures, including crabs and shellfish that tend to live just off the shore in shallow water. Amenities include grills, a picnic area and playground, and restrooms, and the beach is wheelchair-accessible. Lifeguards are on duty daily during the summer season, mid-June to Labor Day. Daytime parking is restricted to town residents in summer, but there is public parking for nonresidents available in the afternoon, when crowds have diminished.

Warren Town Beach

Warren Street, Warren, RI

Located on the Warren River at the end of Warren Street, this small beach is great for kids, and has a pier often used for fishing. Amenities include a playground and restrooms.

Fees: Parking fees during the summer season, June to September.

Brenton Point State Park

Ocean Drive, Newport, RI

This state park offers spectacular views of Rhode Island Sound. Once the grounds of a grand estate, it now offers relaxation and enjoyment for the public. Benches run all along the seawall, making it a good place to sit and relax, but also a good location for fishing, tide-pooling, and beachcombing. It is not recommended for swimming. The beach itself is cobbled, with little access for sunbathing or lounging. If you want to sunbathe or picnic, it's best done from the grassy area around the seawall.

Fees: Parking fee.

Fort Adams State Park

Harrison Avenue, Newport, RI

The park is located at the mouth of Newport Harbor. It offers a large number of activities, including fishing, swimming, boating, and shell collecting. It's also the site of the Newport Jazz and Folk Festival. The small rocky beach area at the tip of the park is not recommended for swimming, but it's a great place for stacking stones and collecting sea glass. This park also has a saltwater swimming beach. There are showers and restrooms available, and most of the site is wheelchair-accessible.

Fees: Parking fee; there's also a fee to enter and explore the fort.

Easton's Beach (First Beach)

175 Memorial Boulevard, Newport, RI

First Beach is popular with families, but is usually crowded. It has many amenities, including over-sand wheelchairs. Restrooms and showers are available, and lifeguards are on duty during the summer season, Memorial Day through September. Dogs are permitted on the beach in the off-season, from October to Memorial Day.

Fees: Parking fee.

Sachuest Town Beach (Second Beach)

474 Sachuest Beach Road, Middletown, RI

This town-operated sandy beach is great for shell collecting, and its western end is home to a great example of New England puddingstone. The beach is connected on the east end by the Sachuest Point National Wildlife Refuge, and also has a section of sand dunes. Second Beach is usually less crowded than First Beach. There are showers, a snack bar, changing stations, and restrooms. Lifeguards are on duty during the summer season, Memorial Day to Labor Day, and leashed pets are allowed on the beach after hours, from 5:00 p.m. to 7:45 a.m.

Fees: Seasonal parking stickers required.

Third Beach

Third Beach Road, Middletown, RI

This small, peaceful stretch of beach, often overlooked by summer crowds, lies in a protected cove just north of Sachuest Point. It's a great place for hiking and nature walks, and has calm waters ideal for children. Third Beach is down the road from Second Beach in Middletown, tucked away behind a salt marsh. There's a picnic area, and fishing is allowed in designated areas. Other amenities include a boat ramp, restrooms, and kayak rentals. Lifeguards are on duty during the summer season, Memorial Day to Labor Day, and dogs are allowed on a leash.

Fees: Admission charged, but free parking.

Sandy Point Beach

Sandy Point Avenue, Portsmouth, RI

You'll find this beach at the end of Sandy Point Avenue to be another great place to take kids. Located on the Sakonnet River, it offers a shallow, quiet alternative to ocean beaches. There are restrooms and changing rooms available, and lifeguards are on duty during the summer season, Memorial Day to Labor Day.

Fees: Admission fee for nonresidents.

Narragansett Town Beach

39-81 Boston Neck Road (Route 1A), Narragansett, RI

This half-mile beach is located in the center of Narragansett. It has calm waves and is family-oriented, with many seasonal activities, including surfing lessons, aerobics classes, sand-castle contests, and volleyball games. Amenities include lockers, showers, restrooms, cabana rentals, snack bar, picnic area, a pavilion, changing rooms, and a boardwalk. This beach is wheelchair-accessible. Lifeguards are on duty during the summer season, mid-June to Labor Day.

Fees: Parking fee, and admission fee for people entering on foot.

Roger Wheeler State Beach

100 Sand Hill Cove Road, Narragansett, RI

This state beach is also known as Sand Hill Cove Beach. It's a popular spot to take young children, and is fully protected by numerous breakwaters. Amenities include a picnic area, restrooms, snack bar, swing set, a large parking area, and wheelchair access. Lifeguards are on duty during the summer season, Memorial Day to Labor Day. No pets are allowed on the beach.

Fees: Free beach entry, but variable parking fees.

Salty Brine State Beach

254 Great Island Road, Narragansett, RI

Salty Brine State Beach, once known as Galilee State Beach, is a clean, sandy beach with gentle surf protected by a breakwater. Its gradual slope makes it an appropriate beach for children. It's a great location for swimming, and there's ample opportunity for fishing, especially along the breakwater. On our visit we found lots of shells, including surf clams and whelks. Amenities include restrooms, a pavilion, a boardwalk along the jetty, shade areas for those who need to get out of the sun, a concession stand, coin-operated hot showers, a lifeguard tower, and ample parking. Lifeguards are on duty daily during the summer season, Memorial Day to Labor Day.

Fees: Free beach entry, but variable parking fees.

Scarborough State Beaches (North and South)

870-970 Ocean Road, Narragansett, RI

Scarborough State Beach is a clean, sandy beach with moderate to heavy surf and an occasional strong undertow. North Beach is located just south of Black Point along Ocean Road, and offers an excellent opportunity for surfing, both body- and board. The large parking area, along with bus drop-off services, allows ample access to both beaches. Amenities include a pavilion, picnic area, restrooms, snack bar, showers, boardwalk with gazebos, and wheelchair access. Lifeguards are on duty daily during the summer season, Memorial Day to Labor Day.

Fees: Free beach entry, but variable parking fees.

Fogland Beach / Tiverton Town Beach

Fogland Beach Road, Tiverton, RI

Fogland Beach offers an unobstructed view of the Sakonnet River and Portsmouth shoreline, and provides an excellent location for windsurfing. The cove area to the north of the beach provides a number of opportunities for nature study. Amenities include changing rooms, showers, restrooms, and a children's playground. Pets are not allowed. Lifeguards are on duty during the summer season, June to September.

Fee: Free beach entry, but variable parking fees.

Grinnell's Beach

Main Road and Lawton Avenue, Tiverton, RI

This small, family-oriented beach on the Sakonnet River offers easy access to the shore and facilities. Gray's Ice Cream, located nearby, is a popular spot for summer refreshment. Amenities include a playground, changing rooms, and restrooms. Lifeguards are on duty during the summer season, June to September. Pets are not allowed.

Fees: Variable parking fees.

MASSACHUSETTS
Horseneck Beach State Reservation

5 John Reed Road, Westport, MA

Horseneck Beach is a barrier beach located in Westport, and one of the most popular sites in the state system. The beach faces Buzzards Bay, and is great for windsurfing, fishing, swimming, and camping. When the currents are favorable there is also ample opportunity for shell collecting. There are one hundred camping sites, and because of its proximity to an extensive estuary system, this is a prime bird-watching location. The beach is wheelchair-accessible. No pets allowed.

Fees: Variable parking fees.

Apponagansett Town Beach

77 Gulf Road, Dartmouth, MA

This is a sandy beach with amenities that include a picnic area, playground, parking, and food concessions. The park is open year-round to the public, and lifeguards are on duty during the summer season, from July through Labor Day.

Fees: Parking fee.

Demarest Lloyd Memorial State Park

Barney's Joy Road, Dartmouth, MA

Demarest Lloyd is an 1,800-foot-long sandy beach, located off the beaten path, at the end of Barney's Joy Road. It's a quieter beach, as most people head to Horseneck Beach, to the west. This ocean beach is located on Buzzards Bay, and it's a great place for kids. There's also a large saltwater marsh excellent for birding enthusiasts. Water temperatures can be warmer than other beaches in the area because of the calm, shallow surf. Lifeguards are on duty during the summer season, Memorial Day to Labor Day.

Fees: Parking fee.

Onset Beach

Onset Avenue, Wareham, MA

Onset Beach is a sandy beach on Buzzards Bay. Amenities include concession stands and restrooms. Lifeguards are on duty during the summer season, Memorial Day to Labor Day.

Fees: Parking fee.

Monument Beach

Emmons Road, off Shore Road, Bourne, MA

Monument Beach is on tiny Toby's Island in Buzzards Bay. Amenities include a boardwalk, snack bar, restrooms, wheelchairs, windsurfing, bathhouse, and a large parking lot. Lifeguards are on duty during the summer season, from June to September.

Fees: Parking sticker required. Sticker may be purchased from the town with proof of a minimum of thirty-day residency within the town. All others welcome to walk or bicycle to the beach.

Old Silver Beach

Off Route 28A and Quaker Road, North Falmouth, MA

This beach is located on Buzzards Bay and is a pleasant beach for swimming. The water is clear, the bottom is clean, and there's a sandbar at low tide, making it a great place for kids to dig and explore. The beach is divided: One side is the public beach, and fills up quickly in the summer, and the other side is reserved for town residents. Amenities include restrooms, a bathhouse, food concessions, beach wheelchairs, and a ramp to the beach. Lifeguards are on duty during the summer season, Memorial Day to Labor Day.

Fees: Nonresidents who are staying at a lodging in the town of Falmouth may purchase a beach sticker for access to the town beach.

Surf Drive Beach

Surf Drive, off Main and Shore Streets, Falmouth, MA

This beach is located on Vineyard Sound and is accessible from the Shining Sea bike path. It's the closest beach to downtown Falmouth, and it offers fine sand, full sun, and a spectacular view of the ocean and Martha's Vineyard. Amenities include restrooms, a concession stand, bathhouse, beach wheelchairs, and a ramp to the beach. Lifeguards are on duty during the summer season, Memorial Day to Labor Day.

Fees: Nonresidents who are lodging in the town of Falmouth may purchase a beach sticker at the bathhouse on Surf Drive. Parking pass is a daily pass.

Menauhant Beach

Menauhant Road, East Falmouth, MA

This is a long, fairly narrow beach located in a quiet neighborhood of Falmouth, and is divided into an east side and a west side by a tidal stream connecting Bourne's Pond to Vineyard Sound. The beach has a number of parking areas, exhibits moderate wave action, and is broken up with numerous small jetties. The southern end of the beach is home to Falmouth's famous Casino Wharf. Amenities include a bathhouse, mobile snack bar, porta-johns, ramp, and beach wheelchairs. Lifeguards are on duty during summer season, June to September

Fees: Daily parking fee.

South Cape Beach State Park

Great Oak Road, Mashpee, MA

South Cape Beach is a great swimming area. The site is wedged between Vineyard Sound and a saltwater bay. It has a barrier beach and dunes, a salt marsh, pine woodlands, and small freshwater ponds. This white-sand beach, more than a mile long, faces Vineyard Sound. Dune boardwalks, a small parking area, and restrooms are provided. The park is part of the Waquoit Bay National Estuarine Research Reserve. Amenities include over-the-dune boardwalks, a small parking area, and restrooms. Interpretive programs are offered during the summer months. Lifeguards are on duty during the summer season, Memorial Day to Labor Day.

Fees: A parking fee is charged during the regular season.

Veterans Park

Ocean Street, Hyannis, MA

Located on Lewis Bay, the beach area has swings and picnic tables in a shaded pine grove. This is a great location for picnics and for those who don't necessarily visit the beach for the sun. Amenities include restrooms, bathhouse, and concession stand. The beach has wheelchair access, and lifeguards are on duty daily during the summer season, Memorial Day to Labor Day.

Fees: Parking sticker is required. Fee for nonresident parking sticker is by the day, week, or for the season. Daily permit may be purchased at the beach; weekly and seasonal permits must be purchased at the National Guard Armory, 225 South Street, Hyannis.

Kalmus Park

Ocean Street, Hyannis, MA

This beach is located in Hyannis Harbor on Nantucket Sound, at Dunbar Point, and is operated by the town of Barnstable. A sandy beach, it ends abruptly at a long breakwater. It has its fair share of seaweed at times. This beach is popular for windsurfing, and amenities include bathhouse, picnic area, and concession stand. The beach has wheelchair access, and lifeguards are on duty during the summer season, Memorial Day to Labor Day.

Fees: Parking permit is required. Fee for nonresident parking sticker is by the day, week, or for the season. Daily permit may be purchased at the beach.

Sea Street / Keyes Beach

Sea Street, Hyannis, MA

This sandy beach is located in Hyannis Harbor on Nantucket Sound, and is close to Hyannis businesses and accommodations. The calm surf here makes it a good spot to spend the day with family and friends. Amenities include a bathhouse, picnic area, grills, and a concession stand. The beach has wheelchair access, and lifeguards are on duty daily during the summer season, Memorial Day to Labor Day.

Fees: Fee for nonresident parking sticker is by the day, week, or for the season. Daily permit may be purchased at the beach.

Bass Hole or Gray's Beach

Off Center Street, Yarmouth, MA

This beach on Cape Cod Bay is operated by the town of Yarmouth. The water is calm, and although small, the beach is a good place to bring children. Amenities include a picnic area with grills, a playground, pavilion, restrooms, and parking. It's a good location for fishing and wildlife observation. A boardwalk over an extensive salt marsh and part of the Callery-Darling Conservation Area allows visitors to stand above the marsh and observe crabs and other creatures in their natural environment. The conservation area also has many trails offering walks through wetlands and woods. Lifeguards are on duty during the summer season, Memorial Day to Labor Day.

Fees: Nonresident beach sticker fee.

Bass River (Smuggler's) Beach

South Shore Drive, Yarmouth, MA

Bass River Beach is gated and closed to the public from 10 p.m. until 8 a.m. Located on Nantucket Sound, it is a clean sandy beach with amenities that include a bathhouse, food concessions, boat ramp including trailer parking, restrooms, and a fishing dock. Locals know this as Smuggler's Beach. Water temperatures are comfortable for New England, and the beach is wheelchair-accessible. Beach wheelchairs are available. Lifeguards are on duty during the summer season, Memorial Day to Labor Day.

Fees: Nonresident beach sticker fees.

Bay View Beach

Bayview Street, Yarmouth, MA

Town-operated Bay View Beach is located on Lewis Bay at the end of Bayview Street. The beach is wheelchair-accessible and has restroom facilities, but there are no lifeguards on duty. Open for the summer season, Memorial Day to Labor Day.

Fees: Nonresident beach sticker fees.

Seagull Beach

South Shore Drive, Yarmouth, MA

This beach on Nantucket Sound is run by the town of Yarmouth, and is their largest beach. It's a good place for collecting shells, and its small waves make it a good beach for swimming. Amenities include large parking area, dunes, snack bar, beach wheelchairs, deck onto the beach, showers, and a concession stand. Lifeguards are on duty during the summer season, Memorial Day to Labor Day.

Fees: Nonresident beach sticker fees are by the day, week, or for the season. Seasonal beach stickers are available at the Yarmouth Town Hall, 1146 Route 28, South Yarmouth.

Seaview Beach

South Shore Drive, Yarmouth, MA

If you're looking for a small, quiet beach where you can relax and reflect, Seaview Beach is a good choice. Overlooking Nantucket Sound, this beach's amenities include restrooms, a seawall, boardwalk, and picnic area. There are no lifeguards on duty.

Fees: Nonresident beach sticker fees are for the day, week, or season. Seasonal beach stickers are available at the Yarmouth Town Hall, 1146 Route 28, South Yarmouth.

Parker's River Beach

South Shore Drive, Yarmouth, MA

This town-operated beach is located on Nantucket Sound and has a large parking area. Amenities include a playground, bathhouse, restrooms, food concessions, and a pavilion. Beach wheelchairs are available. Lifeguards are on duty during the summer season, Memorial Day to Labor Day.

Fees: Nonresident beach sticker fees are for the day, week, or season. Seasonal beach stickers are available at the Yarmouth Town Hall, 1146 Route 28, South Yarmouth, and at the Chamber of Commerce, 424 Route 28, West Yarmouth.

Englewood Beach

Berry Avenue, Yarmouth, MA

This beach is located at the end of Berry Avenue, where you'll find a small parking lot, a jetty that is good for fishing, and a marina. High tide covers much of this beach, and there are no lifeguards on duty.

Fees: Nonresident beach sticker fees apply. Seasonal beach stickers (Memorial Day to Labor Day) are available at the Yarmouth Town Hall, 1146 Route 28, South Yarmouth.

West Dennis Beach

Off Lighthouse Inn Road, West Dennis, MA

This family-oriented beach is located on Nantucket Sound. The western end is public, and the eastern end is designated for town residents only. Amenities include restrooms, paid parking, concession stand, showers, and wheelchair access. Lifeguards are on duty daily during the summer season, Memorial Day to Labor Day.

Fees: Nonresidents and people who are not lodging in Dennis may buy a beach pass at the beach for the day, which can be used that day at all public beaches. Nonresidents may buy a weeklong beach pass at Dennis Town Hall, 485 Main Street.

Chapin Memorial Beach

Chapin Beach Road, Dennis, MA

Chapin Memorial Beach is located on Cape Cod Bay. At low tide the beach has wide tidal flats, making it a great place to take a stroll. There are restrooms at the beach, but few other amenities. This is a good beach for shell collecting, observing nature, and enjoying the sun. The summer season is from Memorial Day to Labor Day, but no lifeguards are on duty.

Fees: Nonresidents and people who are not lodging in Dennis may buy a beach pass at the beach, which can be used that day at all public beaches.

Mayflower Beach

Dunes Road, Dennis, MA

Stunning Mayflower Beach is a favorite for families. Located on Cape Cod Bay, the beach has a long boardwalk from the parking lot to the beach across the dunes. The sand is soft, and at low tide the sandbars are endless. There are many tidal pools for kids to explore, and the clean, clear water is seaweed-free. Amenities include restrooms, concession stands, and wheelchair access. Lifeguards are on duty during the summer season, Memorial Day to Labor Day.

Fees: Nonresidents and people who are not lodging in Dennis may buy a beach pass at the beach for the day, which can be used that day at all public beaches. Nonresidents may buy a weeklong beach pass at Dennis Town Hall, 485 Main Street.

Corporation Beach

Corporation Road, Dennis, MA

This is another town beach located on the bay side of the town of Dennis. Here you'll find warm, calm waters for swimming, fine sand, and large sandy tidal flats at low tide, conducive to walking. Amenities include a snack bar, restrooms, play area, and wheelchair access. Lifeguards are on duty during the summer season, Memorial Day to Labor Day.

Fees: Nonresidents and people who are not lodging in Dennis may buy a beach pass at the beach.

Red River Beach

Off Uncle Venie's Road, Harwich, MA

Red River Beach is located on Nantucket Sound and is the largest beach in Harwich. There are no concession stands, but the ice-cream truck makes frequent stops here. This is a good place to launch kayaks and for windsurfing. There aren't many amenities at this beach, but there are restrooms, and lifeguards are on duty during the summer season, Memorial Day to Labor Day. **Fees:** A daily parking pass (available at the beach) is required between 9 a.m. and 5 p.m.

Ridgevale Beach

Ridgevale Road, Chatham, MA

This ocean beach on Nantucket Sound between Harding's and Cockle Cove Beach is great for families and kids. You can explore the tidal areas, and the small waves make it a good place for kids to swim, although it can be a little weedy at times. Amenities include restrooms and a concession stand. Lifeguards are on duty daily during the summer season, Memorial Day to Labor Day. **Fees:** Beach access is free to those walking or on bikes; stickers are required for parking. Parking passes (available at the beach) are required between 9 a.m. and 5 p.m. Daily fee for parking.

Chatham Lighthouse Beach

Shore Road, Chatham, MA

Chatham's Lighthouse Beach is open year-round and has become a destination spot in recent years for a new local summer guest, the great white shark. The beach was formed years ago because of a break in the Great Barrier Beach. It is protected from heavy surf by Nauset Beach, but beware of tidal currents; they can be very strong. The beach has fine-sand dunes and wonderful panoramic views. There are daily sightings of seals and, in recent years, great white sharks. The beach can be reached by shuttle, on foot, or bicycle. There is a small parking area that fills up quickly and has a thirty-minute limit, so you shouldn't plan on adjacent parking. Beachgoers can park on Main Street in the downtown and take a taxi or shuttle to the beach. Be prepared for a half-mile walk across the sand. There are no restrooms, lifeguards, or concessions.

Cockle Cove

Off Cockle Cove Road, Chatham, MA

This town-managed beach is located on Nantucket Sound and is a good place for kids. Its calm, protected shoreline and shallow waters make it a great swimming beach, and it offers an enjoyable place for walking, shell collecting, and observing nature. It's also a good location for windsurfers and kayakers. Restrooms are available, and lifeguards are on duty during the summer season, from June to September.

Fees: Various parking fees. A parking pass is required, and available at the beach tollbooth. Nonresidents must purchase passes with cash at the booth.

Harding's Beach

Harding's Beach Road, off Barn Hill Road, Chatham, MA

Harding's Beach is located on Nantucket Sound in protected waters, along Chatham's southern coast. This is a great beach to launch a sailboat or kayaks for a day on the water, or to spend time hiking along many of the trails behind the beachfront, collecting shells and beach stones. It's also ideal for swimming and sunbathing. Amenities include two parking lots, a bathhouse, showers, and food trucks. Lifeguards are on duty during the summer season, Memorial Day to Labor Day.

Fees: Beach stickers for nonresident parking can only be purchased with cash at the on-site beach booth, or at the Chatham Permit Department, 283 George Ryder Road, Chatham.

Nauset Beach

Beach Road, Orleans, MA

Nauset Beach is a broad ocean beach with massive sand dunes, big ocean waves, and chilly water. It is operated by the town of Orleans, and shouldn't be confused with nearby Nauset Light Beach of the Cape Cod National Seashore. Off-road vehicles are allowed, but permits must be obtained through the town of Orleans. Amenities include restrooms and food concessions. Lifeguards are on duty during the summer season, from mid-June to Labor Day.

Fees: Daily parking fees may be purchased at the beach. Parking stickers by the week and for the season may be purchased at the Nauset Beach Administration Building. There is a variable fee scale based on residency.

Skaket Beach

Skaket Beach Road, Orleans, MA

Skaket Beach is located on Cape Cod Bay and offers calm waters usually warmer than the oceanside beaches. I enjoy this beach the most at low tide, with its expansive tidal flats offering an opportunity for exploration in its many tide pools. This is also a popular beach from which to watch the sunset over the bay. Amenities include restrooms, a concession stand, and wheelchair access, and lifeguards are on duty during the summer season, from mid-June to Labor Day.

Fees: Daily parking pass may be purchased at the beach; free parking in late afternoon. Parking stickers by the week and for the season may be purchased at the Nauset Beach Administration Building.

Eastham, Wellfleet, Truro, and Provincetown, MA (Cape Cod National Seashore)

Cape Cod National Seashore manages six ocean beaches in the following towns: Eastham (Coast Guard and Nauset Light beaches), Wellfleet (Marconi Beach), Truro (Head of the Meadow Beach), and Provincetown (Herring Cove and Race Point beaches). All seashore beaches include showers, paved parking, restrooms, changing rooms, drinking water, and lifeguards (late June through Labor Day). Two beaches, Coast Guard in Eastham and Herring Cove in Provincetown, are wheelchair-accessible and offer over-sand wheelchairs. Parking lots are open daily, year-round, 6 a.m. to midnight. Lifeguards are at swimming beaches from late June through August.

Fees: Parking fees are required from late June through Labor Day at all six beaches.

Coast Guard Beach (Cape Cod National Seashore)

Doane Road, Eastham, MA

Coast Guard Beach is a beautiful sand beach located on the ocean side of Cape Cod, and is part of the Cape Cod National Seashore. It has soft, deep sand and large, impressive dunes. During the summer season the best way to reach the beach is by the shuttle that leaves the park visitor center throughout the day. Amenities include this shuttle service, showers, and restrooms. The beach is next to the Nauset Marsh and the Nauset Spit, both of which are great locations to view birds and other wildlife. You're sure to see seals, especially along the Nauset Spit, which is a barrier beach, excellent for surf fishing and shell collecting. Lifeguards are on duty daily in designated swimming areas during the summer season, Memorial Day to Labor Day.

Nauset Light Beach (Cape Cod National Seashore)

Ocean View Drive, Eastham, MA

Nauset Light Beach is an iconic Cape Cod beach, often showing up in calendars and on seafood-shack place mats. It's part of the Cape Cod National Seashore and consists of a broad, sandy beach that includes a steep cliff and, of course, historic Nauset Light. The lighthouse has been moved numerous times because of cliff erosion, the last time in 1996. A boardwalk and stairs allow visitors to get down to the beach. Amenities include restrooms open seasonally, parking, and wheelchair access. Lifeguards are on duty during the summer season, from late June to early September.

Fees: Daily parking fee.

Marconi Beach (Cape Cod National Seashore)

Off Route 6 South, Wellfleet, MA

Marconi Beach—also referred to as Marconi Station—is the site made famous in 1903 when Guglielmo Marconi completed the first transatlantic wireless communication between the United States and England. Today, the site offers a superb viewing area across this portion of the Cape from ocean to bay. The beach is also famous for its steep sand cliffs located just behind the beach, and as the general location of "Black Sam" Bellamy's pirate ship, the *Whydah*, wrecked in shoal waters off Cape Cod in 1717. The uplands above the beach slope gradually westward, and offer yet another hidden attraction, a white cedar forest that includes a boardwalk for visitors.

Fees: Daily parking fee.

Head of the Meadow Beach (Cape Cod National Seashore)

Route 6 to Head of the Meadow Road, Truro, MA

This is an ocean beach with strong surf and moving sandbars, because of drift. The beach is secluded, but has restrooms and lifeguards, who are on duty during the summer season, from mid-June to Labor Day. The beach is managed by the town of Truro and the Cape Cod National Seashore.

Fees: Parking sticker is not required; daily parking fee is per day, per car.

Herring Cove (Cape Cod National Seashore)

End of Route 6, Provincetown, MA

The shoreline here drops off dramatically, allowing whales to come close to shore. Amenities include restrooms, concessions, and wheelchair access. Lifeguards are on duty during the summer months from June to September.

Fees: Parking fee.

Race Point Beach (Cape Cod National Seashore)

Race Point Road, Provincetown, MA

This ocean beach has heavy surf and a strong current. The undertow can be powerful at this beach, so it's not recommended for weak swimmers. This is a popular beach for fishing and a great place to see whales and other ocean creatures. The shoreline drops off markedly and whales can be seen close to shore. Amenities include restrooms, showers, and a large parking lot. Lifeguards are on duty during the summer season, Memorial Day to Labor Day.

Fees: Parking costs per day. Seasonal over-sand vehicle permits can be purchased at Race Point Beach from April 10 through November 15. There are various restrictions, and all vehicles must be inspected before the permit is granted.

Corn Hill Beach

Corn Hill Road (from Castle Road), Truro, MA

This sandy beach is located on the bay side of Cape Cod, and has lots of space for walking, especially when the tide is out. Although it feels as though you could almost walk across the bay at certain times, of course, you can't. This is a great beach for swimming and shell collecting, with lots of oyster shells, since the bay is home to oyster farming. The water is calm and somewhat warmer than other Massachusetts beaches that don't receive the effects of the Gulf Stream. This is a good choice for those who want to do some shell fishing, once you've purchased your permit, or to spend time with the kids, exploring tide pools. There are restrooms available, but not much else, which isn't necessarily a bad thing. It's open to the public, but there are no lifeguards or concession stands.

Fees: Parking from June to Labor Day.

Ballston Beach

Route 6 to South Pamet Road, Truro, MA

Ballston is a high-duned, coastal Atlantic beach that often has heavy surf and a dangerous undertow. It boasts beautiful scenery, including many beach creatures; in fact, I've seen seals pretty much every time I've visited this beach. Clean, blue ocean water is the standard, and it's a great place to find shells and other drift-line treasures. Although there isn't much, if any, sea glass, there's plenty of magic quartz beach stones to be found. There are no lifeguards or concessions, so swimming is at your own risk.

Fees: Beach parking is only open to Truro residents and vacationing guests, before 4 p.m. during the summer season (third weekend in June to Labor Day). All others must bicycle in. In-town guests may purchase stickers at the town beach office, at 36 Shore Road.

Mayo Beach

Kendrick Avenue, Wellfleet, MA

This quiet beach is located on Cape Cod Bay in downtown Wellfleet. It's a good family beach with a playground, breakwater, and beautiful views of the harbor. There are very few amenities—no lifeguards, restrooms, or snack bar—but services are available nearby. This is one of only three beaches in Wellfleet open to people who are not living or staying in Wellfleet. The other two are Cahoon Hollow Beach and White Crest Beach.

Fees: All beaches other than Cahoon Hollow, White Crest, and Mayo require a town parking sticker, and stickers are sold only to town residents or people staying at lodgings in Wellfleet.

Cahoon Hollow Beach

Cahoon Hollow Road near Ocean View Drive, Wellfleet, MA

Cahoon Hollow Beach is an ocean beach with surf and occasional undertows, one of the most popular beaches on Cape Cod. It's one of only three beaches in Wellfleet open to the public, the other two being Mayo Beach on the bay side and White Crest Beach. It is known for its high dunes and pounding surf. Amenities include restrooms and a snack bar. The beach is also home to the famous Beachcomber Restaurant and Bar, one of the few oceanfront restaurants located on Cape Cod's outer beach. It was originally built in 1897 as a lifesaving station. This windy, cold-water beach is popular with young adults and families and has wheelchair-accessible parking, although it has limited wheelchair access because of the steep, high-duned pathway. Lifeguards are on duty during the summer season, from mid-June to Labor Day. Swimming is recommended in designated areas only.

Fees: Parking fees.

White Crest Beach

Ocean View Drive, Wellfleet, MA

This ocean beach on Cape Cod is operated by the town of Wellfleet. It's a pretty safe bet that you'll find rough wave action here, which makes it an ideal spot for the surf crowd, but not necessarily family vacationers. This beach also has high sand dunes and the wind is almost always blowing. Hang gliders are allowed before 9 a.m. and after 5 p.m. Amenities include restrooms, a concession stand, and parking. A steep dune path with no stairs leads down to the beach, making it more difficult for older folks and young children to visit. Lifeguards are on duty during the summer season, Memorial Day to Labor Day. This beach does not have wheelchair access.

Fees: Daily parking fee. This is one of only three beaches in Wellfleet open to people who are not living or staying in Wellfleet.

First Encounter Beach

Samoset Road, Eastham, MA

First Encounter Beach is operated by the town of Eastham and is located on the Cape Cod Bay. It is historically significant because it's the site of the first encounter between the Pilgrims, destined to eventually settle in Plymouth, and Native Americans. Its calm waters and sandy flats are great for kids, and the beach shares many of the attributes of other bayside beaches: calm waters, expansive tidal flats, and sand dunes. If you visit in the afternoon, you should stay for the sunset over the bay. There is ample parking and a bathhouse, but no concession stand; however, an ice-cream truck shows up in the parking lot at least twice a day.

Fees: The town of Eastham charges per day for parking. Stickers are available per week, for two weeks, or per season. Stickers can be obtained at the Natural Resources Building at 555 Old Orchard Road, or Sunday only at the First Encounter Beach parking lot.

Breakwater Beach

Breakwater Road off Route 6A, Brewster, MA

This beautiful sandy beach is a popular destination for families with children. Usually not very crowded, it has dunes, tidal flats at low tide, and mild water temperature. The rocky sections are great for tide-pooling, and kids will love searching for the animals and plants that call this place home. The waters are calm, and at low tide you can walk out quite a distance to find even more places to explore. There are no lifeguards, so swimming is at your own risk. Some of the sections are wheelchair-accessible, and restrooms are available.

Fees: Various beach parking permit fees during the summer season, from mid-June to Labor Day.

Sandy Neck Beach

Sandy Neck Road West, Barnstable, MA

Sandy Neck is a large, undeveloped barrier beach on Cape Cod Bay that's managed by the town of Barnstable. Large sand flats are exposed at low tide, making it a great place to explore. The beach is part of a larger natural complex that includes dunes and marshlands, and is a great place for hiking, bird watching, and kayaking. Amenities include restrooms, concession stand, and beach wheelchairs. Lifeguards are on duty daily during the summer season, Memorial Day to Labor Day. Off-road vehicles are allowed on the beach with a seasonal permit.

Fees: Admission fee. Nonresident parking sticker is by the day, week, or for the season. Daily permit may be purchased at the beach.

Craigville Beach

Craigville Beach Road, Barnstable, MA

Craigville Beach is located on Nantucket Sound and is a popular beach for sunbathing and people watching. It's also good for swimming. This beach is clean and family-oriented; the water is warm and the waves are small, unless there's an onshore breeze. Amenities include restrooms and wheelchair access. Lifeguards are on duty during the summer season, Memorial Day to Labor Day.

Fees: Parking permit is required. For beach sticker information, call Barnstable Town Hall.

Scusset Beach

20 Scusset Beach Road, Sandwich, MA

Scusset Beach is located on Cape Cod Bay. It is a popular fishing location, with a pier, breakwater, and frontage along the Cape Cod Canal. The beach also has a camping area, with close to one hundred sites. Amenities include restrooms, showers, picnic area, and concession stand. Lifeguards are on duty during the summer season, Memorial Day to Labor Day.

Fees: Daily parking fee.

Town Neck Beach

Off Wood Avenue, Sandwich, MA

This town-operated beach on Cape Cod Bay has a wonderful, long boardwalk over marshes, a creek, and dunes to the beach. The beach can be rocky at times and not the best place to spread a blanket and catch some sun, but if you're looking for seashells and beach stones, this is the beach for you. It also offers great vistas of the bay. There are no lifeguards on duty, and no restrooms are available.

Fees: Daily parking fees.

Surfside Beach

Surfside Road, Nantucket, MA

Surfside Beach is accessible by public bus and is one of the most popular beaches on Nantucket Island, located at the end of Surfside Road. This is a family beach that offers restrooms, showers, concession stand, and chair and umbrella rentals, and lifeguards on duty during the summer season, June to September. With miles of sand for fishing, having a picnic, flying kites, or swimming, this beach has something for everyone.

Miacomet Beach

End of Miacomet Road, South Shore, Nantucket, MA

Miacomet Beach is known for its heavy surf and rip currents and can be a dangerous place to swim. There is a parking lot but no amenities. Lifeguards are *not* on duty at this beach. If you're looking for a more family-friendly beach, you might want to try Miacomet Pond.

Cisco Beach, Hummock Pond Road, Nantucket, MA

Cisco Beach is located on the western side of the island's south shore, at the end of Hummock Pond Road, and is open year-round. Of note is the very soft sand and above-average waves, great for surfing. Of course, this means the surf is very strong and there are often rip currents. Proceed with caution, as there are limited lifeguards on duty and sparse restrooms; you shouldn't count on either.

Francis Street Beach

Francis Street, Nantucket, MA

This sandy beach is not far from downtown, and only about a four-minute walk from Main Street. You can rent kayaks here to further enjoy the calm waters. There are restrooms, but no lifeguards on duty.

Siasconset Beach

5 Gully Road Siasconset, Nantucket, MA

Siasconset Beach is on the eastern tip of Nantucket Island and located close to Sconset Village. The water is rougher than at other beaches because of its location, but it's a beautiful beach. Less crowded than other Nantucket beaches, it's close enough to Sconset for visitors to consider the village an amenity. Parking can be tough, but the beach is on the Nantucket Regional Transit Authority Shuttle route, so there isn't really a need to take a car. Lifeguards are on duty during the summer season, Memorial Day to Labor Day. Amenities include nearby restaurants, and restrooms can be found within walking distance.

Children's Beach (Harbor Beach)

Harbor View Way, Nantucket, MA

Children's Beach is an easy walk from downtown if you follow South Beach Street to Harbor View Way. This is an ideal beach to visit with small children. Amenities include a playground, bandstand, restrooms, showers, concession stands, and picnic tables. Lifeguards are on duty during the summer season, Memorial Day to Labor Day.

Jetties Beach

Bathing Beach Road, Nantucket, MA

Jetties Beach is a short walk from downtown. This is a protected beach with small waves, making it a good choice for families. Amenities include tennis courts, skateboard park, a playground, and restrooms. This is the Nantucket beach that hosts the Boston Pops in the summer. Lifeguards are on duty during the summer season, Memorial Day to Labor Day.

Coskata-Coatue Wildlife Refuge

Wauwinet Road, Wauwinet (on the island of Nantucket), MA

Coskata-Coatue Wildlife Refuge is known for its sand dunes, historic lighthouse, world-class fishing, and 390 acres of barrier beach. The refuge includes sixteen miles of walking trails and beachfront. Gray and harbor seals are common in the surf, and other wildlife abound. Facilities include public restrooms between the Wauwinet Gatehouse and Great Point Lighthouse, and at the lighthouse. The beach is closed from 10 p.m. to 5 a.m., with the exception of fishing.

Fees: Free to all pedestrians.

Dionis Beach

Eel Point Road, Nantucket, MA

Many families like Dionis Beach, located on the western side of Nantucket's north shore. It's considered a remote beach by island standards, and is often loaded with seashells and other drift-line material. Waves are generally small and the beach is very long. Amenities include restrooms, showers, and parking. Lifeguards are on duty during the summer season, mid-June to Labor Day.

Brant Point Beach, Easton Street, Nantucket, MA

Located right at the Brant Point Lighthouse, this is not really a beach for swimming, as there are no lifeguards on duty, or other amenities (meaning, no restrooms). It's a sandy spit of land with strong currents and lots of boat traffic—a nice place to sit and watch the boats go by, or the artists painting their vision of the lighthouse. Instead of swimming, do some shell collecting; this is a great beach for slipper shells, bay scallops, and winkles.

Katama Beach (South Beach)

Katama Road, Edgartown, Martha's Vineyard, MA

This is one of my favorite beaches; if you visit Martha's Vineyard, you really should visit South Beach. It consists of three miles of barrier beach on the island's south shore, at the end of Katama Road. The rough surf here is popular with surfers, but it's also a great beach to just soak up the sun. Whenever I've visited this beach the waves have been powerful, and the drop-off so compelling, that very few people were in the water. Like the southern beaches on Nantucket, this beach has loose, uncompacted sand, making it a chore to walk on at times. Amenities include ample parking, beach shuttle, and some restroom facilities. It's also accessible by bike path. Lifeguards patrol some sections of the beach daily from mid-June to Labor Day.

Fees: Beach is open to all. Vehicles with permits allowed on marked trails.

Oak Bluffs Town Beach

Town Wharf and Steamship Authority dock, Oak Bluffs, Martha's Vineyard, MA

The Oak Bluffs Town Beach offers calm waters and a place to enjoy walking and sunbathing. It can be a little rocky at times, but if you're staying in Oak Bluffs and want to spend a little time at the beach, this one is just a short walk across the street. There are public restrooms at the Steamship Authority parking lot, but no lifeguards patrol this beach, and there are no amenities. This isn't really an issue, though, since the town is right behind you. The beach begins near the Steamship Authority dock and terminates at the first jetty heading toward Edgartown.

Chappy Point Beach

Chappaquiddick Road, Chappaquiddick, MA

Chappy Point is located on Chappaquiddick and adjacent to Edgartown on the island of Martha's Vineyard. The Point has two beaches: one faces the inner harbor, and the other looks toward the outer harbor and Nantucket Sound. These beaches are good for sunbathing and shell collecting, but not recommended for swimming because of the many boats and heavy harbor traffic. You can reach the beach by taking the ferry that crosses the harbor—the one you may remember from the movie *Jaws*.

Lighthouse Beach

Starbuck's Neck Road, off North Water Street, Edgartown, Martha's Vineyard, MA

Lighthouse Beach has gentle waves and is child-friendly, seldom crowded, and just a short walk from North Water Street. This beach offers pleasant swimming conditions and a view of the harbor and lighthouse.

Long Point Wildlife Refuge

Long Point Road, West Tisbury, Martha's Vineyard, MA

Long Point is a great place for bird watchers and nature lovers. Its six hundred acres are open to the public, and the refuge includes woodlands, a sandy beachfront, and sand dunes. Amenities are sparse, but there are restrooms, picnic tables, and bike racks.

Joseph Sylvia State Beach

Beach Road between Oak Bluffs and Edgartown, Martha's Vineyard, MA

This two-mile-long state beach is located on Beach Road and offers mild, friendly waters and a gradual slope, making it a very popular beach for families. The beach also supports a diverse group of nesting birds, including the federally threatened piping plover, the least tern, and the American oystercatcher. Fishing is a popular activity all along this beachfront. Striped bass are present from early May to November, and bonito can be found in large numbers in July and August. There is parking along the roadway, but spots fill up quickly in the summer. The beach is also accessible by bike path. There are lifeguards on duty during the summer season, Memorial Day through Labor Day.

Moshup Beach (Aquinnah Beach)

Aquinnah, Martha's Vineyard, MA

It's a bit of a hike to get to this beach from the parking lot, but it's worth the walk. This half-mile-long beach is located near the Aquinnah Cliffs on the eastern end of the island that was formerly known as Gay Head. It you don't want to drive, you can take the shuttle bus that runs from the other end of the island, routinely dropping people off in the Moshup Beach parking lot. There are restrooms, but they are not located on the beach. You'll find them adjacent to the parking lot.
Fees: Parking fee.

Menemsha Public Beach

Chilmark, Martha's Vineyard, MA

This beach is located on the "quiet side" of Martha's Vineyard, next to Dutcher's Dock at Menemsha Harbor in the village of Chilmark. Amenities include public parking (although very limited), restrooms, and showers, and food and concessions are close by. This quaint, quiet side of the island can be a refreshing contrast to the more-hectic eastern end.

Tisbury Town Beach (Owen Little Way Town Beach)

Owen Little Way, Vineyard Haven, Martha's Vineyard, MA

Just moments away from Vineyard Haven, this small stretch of shorefront is nice for swimming and sunbathing. There's limited parking, but it's right next to town, with access from Main Street. Located next to the Vineyard Haven Yacht Club.

Lobsterville Beach

Lobsterville Road, Aquinnah, Martha's Vineyard, MA

Lobsterville Beach is located on the north side of Martha's Vineyard and has calm waters, making it a good place to take kids. It's a great place to hunt for seashells and sea glass, and also a favorite location for surf fishing. The beach is open to the public, but parking is restricted to residents only. If you want to visit this beach, you'll need to find other means of transportation. There are a number of shuttle bus services and bike rental shops on the island.

White Horse Beach

Rocky Hill Road, Plymouth, MA

This is a public beach with almost nonexistent parking, and the name of the road the beach is on—Rock Hill Road—reveals the rocky character of the beach. There's also a good chance you'll find plenty of seaweed here. While there are no lifeguards or restrooms, the beach is visited during the day by an ice-cream truck.

Ellisville Harbor State Park

State Road Route 3A, Plymouth, MA

Ellisville Harbor State Park offers views of a barrier beach, a sphagnum bog, and meadows. This is a wonderful place for hiking, walking, bird watching, beachcombing, and swimming. In fall and winter, harbor seals can often be seen just offshore. While parking is available, there are no lifeguards or restroom facilities.

Plymouth Beach

Warren Avenue, Plymouth, MA

This is a long barrier beach that begins near Warren Avenue and extends well into Plymouth Harbor. It's a great place for hiking or just lying on the beach and enjoying the summer sun. It's somewhat unique because of its extension into the harbor, with water on both sides and sand dunes in between. Part of the beach is closed during the shorebird nesting season. Dogs are allowed on the beach, but owners must follow a strict schedule. There are beach signs posted explaining times and areas where dogs are allowed. Amenities include parking, restrooms, and a concession stand, all located near the southern end of the beach. Lifeguards are on duty during the summer season, Memorial Day to Labor Day, in designated swimming areas.

Fees: Parking fee.

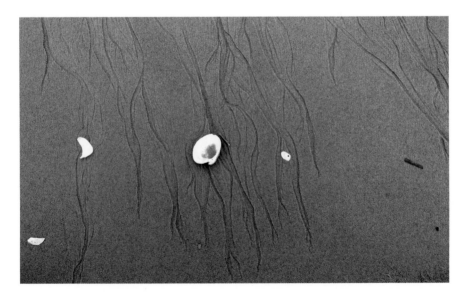

Nelson Street Beach

Water and Nelson Streets, Plymouth, MA

This beach has a wheelchair-accessible recreation area with soccer fields. Amenities include a splash pool and concession stand, but there are no lifeguards on duty and no restroom facilities.
Fees: Parking fee.

Duxbury Beach

Gurnet Road, Duxbury, MA

Duxbury Beach is a six-mile-long barrier beach that juts out into the Atlantic Ocean, making it as unique as its counterpart, Plymouth Beach in Plymouth. Duxbury Beach stretches into the harbor from the north and Plymouth Beach from the south. This one is definitely worth visiting if you're in the area. Parking is available at the entrance. This dune-covered barrier beach is a great place to hike or just sit and enjoy the day. There are no concessions or restroom facilities, but an ice-cream truck visits the parking lot throughout the day. Lifeguards are on duty in designated swimming areas during the summer season, Memorial Day to Labor Day.
Fees: Parking fee.

Brant Rock Beach

Off Dyke Road, Marshfield, MA

This beach has lots of tidal pools with all sorts of marine life for kids to explore. Because the beach is narrow, you may need to move at high tide. There are parking spaces for residents with beach stickers, and nonresidents can buy day passes. Lifeguards are on duty during the summer season, Memorial Day to Labor Day.
Fees: Variable parking rates.

Rexhame Beach

Standish Street, Marshfield, MA

Rexhame is a sandy beach run by the town of Marshfield. It's good for swimming, but pay attention to the shifting currents, as they can be very strong at times. Amenities include a concession stand and restrooms. Lifeguards are on duty during the summer season, Memorial Day to Labor Day.
Fees: Beach stickers and day passes, with variable rates.

Green Harbor Beach

Beach Street, Marshfield, MA

Green Harbor is a long, sandy beach that extends from Green Harbor in Marshfield to Duxbury Beach in Duxbury. This is a great place for long walks and sunbathing. Amenities include restrooms and lifeguards, on duty during the summer season, Memorial Day to Labor Day.

Fees: Variable parking rates at various locations, including forty spaces reserved for nonresidents at the Lobster Pound.

Hummarock Beach, Egypt Beach, Sand Hills Beach, Peggotty Beach

Scituate, MA

These four beaches are located in Scituate and are included together because even though the public can gain access, the beaches are essentially resident-only, with three hundred beach stickers reserved for nonresidents if they want to pay the annual fee. Hummarock, Sand Hills, and Peggotty are sandy, and Egypt Beach is slightly cobbled. All have restrooms, but concessions are off-site.

Sandy Beach

Cohasset, MA

As its name indicates, this is a sandy beach, and also a good place to find sea glass if you search at both ends of the beach. Amenities include parking and restroom facilities, and lifeguards are on duty during the summer season, Father's Day to Labor Day. You must have a resident parking pass to park; the best time for nonresidents to visit is in the off-season.

Fees: Beach access and parking fees.

Gun Rock Beach

Atlantic Avenue, Hull, MA

Gun Rock Beach is a charming little spot with a natural rock ridge that acts as protection from the ocean currents, creating calm waves instead of crashing ones. The sand at this child-friendly beach is soft, and the rocks are a haven for little creatures that are sure to interest children of all ages. Restaurants and small food stands can be found all along the beach. Parking can be found on Atlantic Avenue. Some spots require a resident parking sticker, while others do not. On weekends, parking at the town hall is also open for beachgoers. There are no lifeguards on duty.

Nantasket Beach Reservation

Route 3A, Nantasket Avenue, Hull, MA

City folks have been coming to Nantasket Beach since the mid-1800s, enjoying a break from the summer heat and all the pleasures that a beach has to offer. One of the unique amenities at this beach is the historic Paragon Carousel. Built in 1928 by the Philadelphia Toboggan Company, the carousel has been in operation for more than eighty years. Amenities include restrooms and a bathhouse. Lifeguards are on duty during the summer season, from late June to early September.

Fees: Daily parking fee.

Nickerson Beach

120 Dorchester Street, Quincy, MA

Nickerson Beach is a very small beach that primarily serves the adjacent Squantum residential neighborhood of Quincy. This scenic coastal area, with its extensive salt marsh and mudflats, is attractive to birds and visitors who like to watch them. This beach is owned by the city of Quincy, and most access is by foot or bicycle, although limited curbside parking is available. The area is also accessible via public transportation from the MBTA Red Line's North Quincy station.

Wollaston Beach

Quincy Shore Drive, Quincy, MA

This beach is a little over three miles long. Caddy Park, on the southern end of the beach, has more than fifteen acres of fields and marsh, and includes a play area, lookout tower, and picnic tables. The road parallel to the beach has many seafood restaurants and ice-cream shops to satisfy your hunger. Parking is available along Quincy Shore Drive. The beach can also be reached by taking the MBTA Red Line to Wollaston Station or North Quincy Station.

Quincy Shores Reservation

Quincy Shore Drive, Quincy, MA

This beach, a little over two miles long, is a popular place for swimming. Caddy Park has a play area for kids and many acres of fields and marsh, as well as picnic sites. The site has views of Quincy Bay and 144-acre Squantum Marsh. The reservation may be reached by Boston MBTA trains. Open year-round, dawn to dusk. Amenities include a bathhouse and restrooms.

Carson Beach

William J. Day Boulevard, South Boston, MA

This sandy beach is located in South Boston and a favorite of local Boston neighborhood inhabitants. The beach offers great views of the harbor and good swimming. Amenities include walkways, benches, lighting, shade shelters, landscaping, and a fishing pier along with a picnic area. The beach can be accessed by subway, bus, or by car. Lifeguards are on duty during the summer season, from June to September. The city of Boston is the dramatic backdrop for this beach.

M Street Beach

Day Boulevard, South Boston, MA

M Street Beach is one of three that make up the longest stretch of uninterrupted sand in the Boston area. L Street and Carson Beach are the other two, and together, these three beaches create almost three miles of shoreline. Amenities include a bathhouse, showers, restrooms, shade shelters, and a playground. M Street Beach is adjacent to the home of the "L Street Brownies," who take the plunge into the cold Atlantic every January 1 to raise money for local charities. The beach is wheelchair-accessible, and lifeguards are on duty during the summer season, mid-June to Labor Day. If you drive, you'll find ample free parking near the beach most of the time, but on sunny weekend days we suggest you take public transportation.

Constitution Beach

Orient Heights, East Boston, MA

This is a family-friendly beach in the heart of Boston. Amenities include a bathhouse, picnic area, playground, restrooms, shade shelters, and foot showers. It also has a number of tennis and handball courts. Lifeguards are on duty during the summer season, mid-June to Labor Day.

Winthrop Beach and Short Beach

Winthrop Shore Drive, Winthrop, MA

These beaches are open from dawn to dusk and are located along Winthrop Shore Drive. The beach is a combination of varying degrees of cobbles and sand, depending on what time of year you visit. Lifeguards are on duty during the summer season, from June to September.

Revere Beach

Revere Beach Boulevard, Revere, MA

Revere Beach has miles of shoreline and was once the hub of all the action in the Revere Beach area. It hosted a giant amusement park and all sorts of amenities. Today the beach is a lot quieter, but people still flock to this historic location to relax, sunbathe, and soak in the sights during the summer months. Amenities include a bandstand for concerts, bathhouse, restrooms, shade shelters, and concession stands. It's also home to the world-famous, original Kelly's Roast Beef (since 1951). Revere Beach is very accessible by public transportation, which makes it a popular spot for people from all over the metro Boston area. The beach is open year-round, from dawn to dusk. Lifeguards are on duty during the summer season, from late June to early September.

Lynn Shore and Nahant Beach Reservation

Lynn Shore Drive, Lynn, MA

Long Beach in Lynn offers public swimming, restroom facilities, and lifeguard supervision during July and August. There is a fee for parking at Long Beach from 8 a.m. to 5 p.m. during the summer season. King's Beach offers public swimming, but there is no lifeguard on duty. There's lots of on-street parking along Lynn Shore Drive available for visitors to King's Beach and Red Rock Park. Park headquarters amenities include the Ward Bathhouse, where a visitor center, showers, and restroom facilities are available free of charge. There are no public restrooms at Lynn Shore Reservation. Open year-round, dawn to dusk.
Fees: Parking fee.

Salem Willows

Fort Avenue, Salem, MA

"The Willows," as most people call it, is a jutting land mass that protrudes into Salem Sound, which separates Salem and Beverly Harbors. It's the location of a historic arcade and has a number of sandy, pocket beaches among its granite outcroppings. Amenities include trails, restrooms, picnic tables, ball fields, a playground, and a band shell. Lifeguards are on duty during the summer season, Memorial Day to Labor Day. Parking is free.

Winter Island

Winter Island Road, Salem, MA

Winter Island, owned by the city of Salem, is the location of an old Coast Guard Station that's been turned into a park. It's also the home of Fort Pickering, a Revolutionary-era fort that some believe is haunted. Amenities include a boat ramp, restrooms, picnic tables, a campground, and a small rocky beach area. The island is also the home to the "stone creatures" discussed in the chapter on beach stones. Parking is free, but there's a fee for admission to the park.
Fees: Entrance fee.

Devereux Beach

155 Ocean Avenue, Marblehead, MA

Marblehead's best-known beach is located just before the causeway on Ocean Avenue. The beach is on the ocean side of the causeway, and the sand can be a little "tired" depending on the time of year. The beach is not wide or long, and is bordered by rock outcroppings on the far end. Amenities include a snack bar, restroom facilities, and a shower. Parking is available, and lifeguards are on duty during the summer season, June to Labor Day.

Fees: Parking fee.

Lynch Park

Off Ober Street, Beverly, MA

Lynch Park is a historic park and once the location of the summer White House of President William Taft. There are two beaches at Lynch Park, a mix of sand and rocks. They are both great tide-pooling beaches, and also a good place to look for seashells and sea glass. Amenities include a beautiful rose garden (actually built within the old foundation of the former Taft summer White House), a concession stand, a bandstand for summer concerts, restrooms, and picnic tables. Many activities happen during the summer months, including fireworks on the Fourth of July. Lifeguards are on duty during the summer season, mid-June to Labor Day.

Fees: Parking fee.

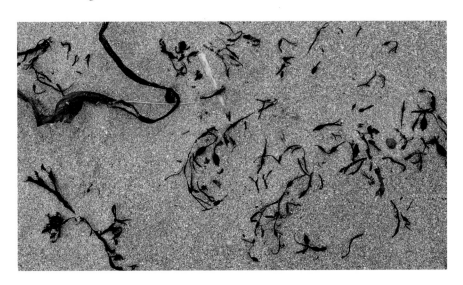

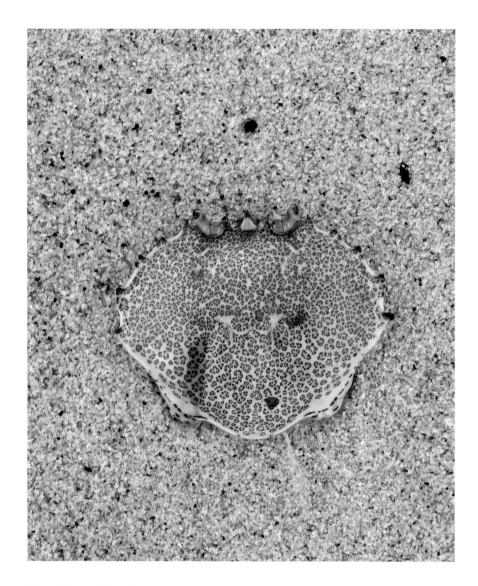

Dane Street Beach

Dane Street, Beverly, MA

This beach is run by the city of Beverly and just down the street from Lynch Park. The beach is a combination of sand and rocks and is a good place to work on one's tan. A small lot offers free parking, but it fills up quickly. Amenities include a bathhouse, restrooms, parking, a play area, and a playground. Dogs are allowed on the beach in the off-season, from Labor Day to Memorial Day.

Singing Beach

Manchester-by-the-Sea, MA

Singing Beach got its name because of the sound the fine, granulated sand makes when you walk on it. This is a good beach for swimming, but also for sunbathing and people watching. The train from Boston stops in the middle of town, and a one-mile walk gets you to the beach. There's parking available, but it's a small lot. Amenities include restrooms, concession stand, showers, and changing rooms. Lifeguards are on duty during the summer season, Memorial Day to Labor Day.

Fees: Parking fee.

Stage Fort Park—Cressy's Beach

Gloucester, MA

This rocky beach is located at historic Stage Fort Park, and overlooks the harbor. Amenities include a large parking area, picnic tables, concession stand, sports fields, playground, cookout areas, restrooms, showers, and changing rooms. Lifeguards are on duty during the summer season, Memorial Day weekend to Labor Day.

Fees: Parking fee.

Half Moon Beach

Stage Fort Park, Gloucester, MA

Half Moon is a quiet pocket beach located in historic Stage Fort Park, and is one of my favorite places to visit in the off-season. This very small beach is surrounded by granite outcroppings on both sides, and gets its name from its crescent shape. Amenities, all located in the park, include restrooms, concession stands, visitor center, grills, and a picnic area. Lifeguards are on duty daily during the summer season, Memorial Day weekend to Labor Day. The beach is wheelchair-accessible, with a concrete ramp leading down to the beach area.

Fees: Parking fee.

Good Harbor Beach

Thatcher Road (Route 127A), Gloucester, MA

Good Harbor is a beautiful beach with lovely white sand facing the Atlantic. At low tide, you can walk out to Salt Island, but pay attention to the tide, or you'll be stranded. A concession stand, showers, and restrooms are located near the parking lot, and the beach is wheelchair-accessible. Lifeguards are on duty daily during the summer season, Memorial Day weekend to Labor Day. The gates open at 8 a.m. and close at 9 p.m. Although the parking lot is big, it does fill up quickly, especially during the weekends.
Fees: Parking fee.

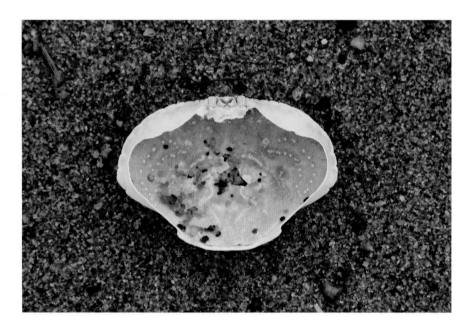

Plum Cove Beach

Washington Street, Gloucester, MA

Located on Washington Street in the northern section of the city, this small, quiet beach has been enjoyed by families in the Lanesville neighborhood for many years. It is a great place to bring small children due to the confines of the beach area. Parking is limited, and restricted to vehicles with a current Gloucester beach sticker. Lifeguards are on duty daily from Father's Day weekend to Labor Day, from 9 a.m. to 5 p.m.

Wingaersheek Beach

Atlantic Avenue, Gloucester, MA

Wingaersheek Beach is located in West Gloucester (before you go over the bridge) and faces the Annisquam River. At low tide the sandbar extends out for a great distance, but be careful of the drop-off near the river, as the current is very strong. Amenities include a concession stand, restrooms, and showers. Lifeguards are on duty during the summer season, Memorial Day to Labor Day. Beach wheelchairs are available. The gates open at 8 a.m. and close at 9 p.m.

Fees: Variable parking fee; rates depend on the day. The parking lot fills up quickly during the summer months, so arrive early if you want to get a space.

Pavilion Beach

Stacey Boulevard, Gloucester, MA

This beach is located within walking distance of downtown Gloucester, on the eastern end of Stacey Boulevard in the area known as "The Fort." During St. Peter's Fiesta, thousands of people watch Gloucester's famous Greasy Pole and seine boat races from Pavilion Beach. The boulevard along Pavilion Beach is also home to the famous Gloucester Fisherman's Memorial. Parking is very limited and there are no restrooms, although the beach is only a short walk from Stage Fort Park and its amenities.

Long Beach

Gloucester and Rockport, MA

Long Beach is a long sandy strand between two granite headlands, and only one headland away from Gloucester's Good Harbor Beach. The beach is noted for its long walkable seawall protecting the private cottages that blanket the elevated shoreline. Long Beach water is cold and clear, with little debris and no drift line to speak of. The public can access the beach from its southern end, and lifeguards are on duty during the summer months, from June to September.

Fees: Parking fee.

Cape Hedge Beach

Route 127, Rockport, MA

Driving on Route 127 toward Rockport, turn right at the Turk's Head Inn and you'll find your way down to a small parking lot for Cape Hedge Beach. Again, unless you're a resident, you'll need a seasonal sticker, and parking here is very limited. However, this beautiful, often undiscovered beach is worth the trip. There are no amenities.

Front Beach

East Main Street, Rockport, MA

Front Beach is a busy place on Sandy Bay, close to downtown. There is only street-metered parking here, so you should park someplace and walk (not easy in Rockport), or have somebody drop you off. If you're really clever, you can drive your car to the Park & Ride lot on Route 127 near the Rockport Information Booth, park, and pay the ridiculously small fee to ride the trolley to the beach. The beach is also within an easy walk from the village of Rockport, for those staying at any of the nearby inns and hotels. There are lifeguards on duty during the summer season, June to September, and public restrooms are available. There are a number of restaurants, eateries, and shops in the area, so you can combine some beach time with browsing and dining.

Crane Beach

Argilla Road, Ipswich, MA

Crane Beach is a gem. Managed by the Trustees of Reservations and connected to the famous Crane Estate, the four miles of fine sand is a great location for swimming, sunbathing, shell collecting, or enjoying a cookout. There's a shipwreck at the eastern end of the beach that can often be seen at low tide.

Amenities include a boardwalk to get beachgoers over the sand dunes, bath-houses, restroom facilities, outdoor showers, picnic tables, bike racks, and a concession stand known as the Crane Beach Store. The large parking lot fills up quickly in the summer months, so go early. Lifeguards are on duty during the summer season, Memorial Day to Labor Day, in designated swimming areas. The beach closes at dusk.

Fees: Entrance fee.

Plum Island

Plum Island, Newburyport, MA

Plum Island offers miles of sandy barrier beach and the Parker River National Wildlife Refuge, home to over eight hundred species of birds, plants, and animals on 4,662 acres. Sandy Point on the southern tip of Plum Island is a state park and a wonderful place to swim, sun yourself, or go tide-pooling. Parking is available at the Refuge, the Point, or in private parking lots.

Salisbury Beach

Beach Road, Route 1A, Salisbury, MA

Salisbury Beach is a large sandy beach with lots of amenities, but also long stretches of undisturbed sand and sea. The beach is four miles long. It's a great place to walk, swim, and collect shells, sea glass, and other interesting souvenirs. The 297-ton, 130-foot, three-masted schooner *Jennie Carter* wrecked on this beach in 1894, and her remains can still be seen just off the beach near the Sea Glass Restaurant. Camping facilities are located at its southern end. Other amenities include bathhouses, restrooms, boardwalks through the dunes, a pavilion, and a playground. Lifeguards are on duty in designated areas, during the summer season, Memorial Day to Labor Day.

Fees: Entrance fee.

NEW HAMPSHIRE
Hampton Beach State Park

160 Ocean Boulevard (Route 1A), Hampton, NH

This long, sandy beach on the Atlantic Ocean provides year-round recreation. The beach can get crowded in the summer months—it's a favorite of vacationing French Canadians—but settles down in the off-season. Activities include swimming, fishing, picnicking, sunbathing, surfing, and recreational vehicle (RV) camping. Amenities include two modern bathhouses—one at the north end, near the Marine Memorial, and the other at the south end, near Haverhill Street. Twenty-eight RV campsites with hookups are available, open for reservations from Memorial Day to Labor Day. Surfers flock to this beach in the summer and fall to catch the waves, and both locals and visitors enjoy many of the walking options along the elevated boardwalk or on the hard-packed sandy beachfront. This is one of the best places for ocean swimming and sunbathing on the short New Hampshire shoreline. Lifeguards are on duty during the summer season, late May through Labor Day.

Fees: Parking fee at South Beach; season passes are available.

North Beach

Route 1A, Hampton, NH

North Beach is a small, sandy, family-friendly beach with less of the frenetic energy of Hampton Beach. It's a great place for swimming and picnicking, or just kicking back and watching the kids play. Amenities include a bathhouse (open year-round) and restrooms. The beach is open weekends in late May, and then daily from June through September. Lifeguards are on duty from mid-June through Labor Day. Pets are not permitted on the beach.

Fees: Parking meters are available along Route 1A, and accept quarters, or tokens can be purchased at the parking lot south of the Hampton Seashell.

Bass Beach / Rye Rocks Point

Rye, NH

When conditions are right, this pebbled beach is a haven for surfers. Located in a cove, it can be difficult to access at times. There is limited parking on the beach side of the road, and there are no amenities.

Jenness Beach State Park

2280 Ocean Boulevard, Rye, NH

Jenness Beach fronts the Atlantic Ocean and is a great place to take the family on a hot summer day. This sandy beach is ideal for swimming and picnicking, and is always open for recreation unless closed or restricted by posting. Amenities at the beach include a bathhouse, open from May 1 through November 1. Lifeguards are on duty during the summer season, late May through Labor Day. Pets are not permitted in the park.

Fees: Metered parking from 8 a.m. to midnight. Parking meters are located along Route 1A and accept quarters.

Odiorne Point State Park

570 Ocean Boulevard (Route 1A), Rye, NH

Odiorne Point State Park offers one of the most beautiful and diverse natural settings along New Hampshire's coastline, with 135 acres of rocky shoreline, sandy beaches, salt marsh, freshwater and saltwater ponds, and dense forest. Military and historical sites at the park are connected by an extensive trails system. Amenities include walking paths, restrooms, the Seacoast Science Center, concession stand, large parking area, picnic areas, and the historic fort. The beach is rocky and a great place for tide-pooling. Kids love this park because there's lots of space to explore and discover. This is a cold-water beach and not great for swimming, but there are plenty of other things to do, like collecting shells and beach stones. If you really want to take a swim, you can always walk next door for a dip in the ocean. Lifeguards are on duty during the summer season, late May through Labor Day. Stone stacking is a big activity at this rocky location. It's also the site of an ancient submerged forest that can often be seen at low tide. Pets are not allowed in the park.

Fees: Admission fee.

Wallis Sands State Beach

1050 Ocean Boulevard (Route 1A), Rye, NH

Wallis Sands is a seven-hundred-foot sandy beach popular with families who aren't interested in restaurants, shops, and arcades. It's also a popular fishing area. Beach amenities include a store that sells a variety of items, food and drinks, and a large bathhouse with hot and cold showers. The park has a grassy area with picnic tables, but fires are not allowed. There is a large parking area, and lifeguards are on duty during the summer season, late May through Labor Day. Pets are not allowed on the beach.

Fees: Admission is per passenger vehicle. New Hampshire residents age sixty-five and over are admitted free. Season passes are available.

MAINE
Fort Foster Beach

Pocahontas Road, Kittery, ME

Fort Foster is a town-managed park, and has three small sandy beaches. This World War II fort has a number of hiking trails and is wheelchair-accessible. Amenities include a pavilion, picnic area, cooking grills, and restrooms. Dogs are allowed on a leash. The park is open year-round from dawn to dusk. Although we've never explored this beach, it has all the ingredients of a very good place to find sea glass.

Fees: The beach is open dawn to dusk, but the gate opens at 10 a.m. and closes at 8 p.m. There are variable entrance fees depending on whether you enter the park by car or bicycle, or on foot.

Long Sands Beach

Route 1A, Cape Neddick, York, ME

Long Sands is a mile and a half of flat, sandy beach located in York. The beach is open seven days a week, twenty-four hours a day, and amenities include restrooms, raft and umbrella rentals, concessions and food venues across the street, and wheelchair accessibility. Surfing is allowed in designated areas, and lifeguards are on duty daily during the summer season, the last week in June through Labor Day. Dogs are allowed on the beach between 6 p.m. and sunrise.
Fees: Various parking fees, at both public and private locations.

Cape Neddick Beach (Passaconaway Beach)

Shore Road, Cape Neddick Village in York, ME

This is a very small beach with limited parking and no facilities. At low tide there are numerous tide pools and a sandbar for exploration. Dogs are allowed on the beach after 6 p.m. There are no lifeguards at this beach.

Harbor Beach

US Route 1, York, ME

Harbor Beach is a sandy pocket beach, open seven days a week but with limited parking. Amenities include restrooms, wheelchair accessibility, and lifeguards on duty from the last week in June through Labor Day. Dogs are allowed on the beach from 6 p.m. to sunrise. From mid-September to mid-May, dogs are allowed on the beach unleashed with the owner present.
Fees: Parking fee.

Short Sands Beach

Ocean Avenue, York, ME

Short Sands beach is open seven days a week, twenty-four hours a day. It's a family-friendly beach with public and private parking available, outside showers, and a playground. Lifeguards are on duty during the summer season, from the last week in June through Labor Day. The beach is wheelchair-accessible, and shops, concession stands, and restaurants are located nearby. Dogs may be on the beach on a leash from 6 p.m. to sunrise. This beach is the home of a shipwreck that shows itself from time to time when the beach loses enough sand.
Fees: Parking fee.

Ogunquit Beach, Footbridge Beach, North Beach

Beach Street, Ogunquit, ME

Ogunquit Beach is three and a half miles of sandy beach and considered one of the premier beaches to visit in Maine. Amenities include restrooms, concession stand, outside showers, picnic tables, chairs and umbrella rentals, and floats. There's a large lot for parking and a ramp to launch boats. Lifeguards are on duty daily during the summer season, mid-June through Labor Day. The middle section of this long barrier beach is known as Footbridge Beach, which you access via a footbridge over the Ogunquit River. The far northern end of the beach is known as North Beach. All three sections have ample parking, lifeguards, and restrooms.

Fees: Parking fee.

Wells Beach

Wells, ME

Wells Beach is more than two miles of smooth sandy beach backed by sand dunes and beach grass. The Wells Beach Jetty is a popular walkway for anglers and children to explore. The parking lot fills up quickly, so try to arrive early. Dogs are allowed on the beach at certain times, but make sure you check the schedule if you plan to bring your dog for a run. Amenities include restrooms, parking, concession stands, a playground, arcade, picnic area, and many nearby shops. The main section of the beach extends to the Wells Beach Jetty. Lifeguards are on duty during the summer season, June through September.
Fees: Parking fee.

Drakes Island Beach

Route 1, Wells, ME

Drakes Island Beach is located just north of Wells Beach, on Route 1. Amenities include parking and restrooms, but no concession stands. This beach is usually less crowded than Wells Beach. Lifeguards are on duty during the summer season, June through September.
Fees: Parking

Goose Rocks Beach

Kings Highway, Kennebunkport, ME

Goose Rocks Beach is three miles of sandy shoreline. Dogs are allowed, but only before 8 a.m. and after 6 p.m. No facilities are available. Parking permits for Goose Rocks Beach are available at the Kennebunk/Kennebunkport Chamber of Commerce, Kennebunkport Town Office, and Kennebunkport Police Department and Goose Rocks General Store.
Fees: Parking fee.

Kennebunk Beaches: Mother's Beach, Pebble Beach, Gooch's Beach

Beach Avenue, Kennebunk, ME

These three beaches are found along Beach Avenue in Kennebunk. Just below Lord's Point is a seven-hundred-foot-long sandy pocket beach known as Mother's Beach. Amenities include restrooms and a playground. There isn't a lot of parking, which is all permit-only. North of Mother's is Pebble Beach, and as the name indicates, this 1,200-foot beach is cobbled. There's a sidewalk and seawall that runs the length of the beach. And finally, just north of Pebble Beach is Gooch's Beach. This 3,960-foot-long stretch of sand is the most popular beach in Kennebunk. All three beaches have restrooms, and lifeguards are on duty during the summer season, July through Labor Day.

Fees: Parking fee. Parking permits are required at all of these beaches, and are available at the Kennebunk chamber of commerce, town hall, and police department.

Fortune's Rocks Beach

Fortune's Rocks Road, Biddeford, ME

Fortune's Rocks is a two-mile-long sandy ocean beach located in Biddeford, offering lots of room to enjoy the summer sun and hard-packed sand. There are no facilities at this beach, and limited parking, but lifeguards are on duty during the summer season, June to September.

Fees: Parking is by permit, available at the Biddeford City Hall clerk's office, 205 Main Street.

Ferry Beach State Park

85 Bayview Road, Saco, ME

Ferry Beach State Park is located off Maine's Route 9 on Bayview Road, between Old Orchard Beach and Camp Ellis, in Saco. The beach is on the southern end of Old Orchard Beach, and there are no lifeguards on duty. After a swim at the beach or a walk on the park's nature trails, you can choose a table and grill in the picnic area. Parking is also available a short walk from the beach, and there are restrooms and changing rooms for your comfort. At nearby Ocean Park, you can take a hike and explore the salt-marsh ecosystem, part of the Rachel Carson National Wildlife Refuge. The park is open from Memorial Day to Columbus Day. Dogs are not allowed on the beach from April 1 to September 30.

Fees: Entrance fee.

Old Orchard Beach

Grand Avenue, Old Orchard Beach, ME

Old Orchard Beach is a seven-mile-long, wide, hard-packed sandy beach, and is Maine's most popular beach. Just across from the beach are arcades, amusement rides, restaurants, concession stands, gift shops, and lodging of all kinds. Old Orchard Beach also features the five-hundred-foot-long "Pier," an icon since 1898. The beach is a perfect spot to sunbathe, walk, people-watch, and swim. The beach also hosts numerous festivals, fairs, free concerts, street dances, and weekly fireworks. Parking is available in and around Old Orchard Beach at several municipal lots and many privately operated ones. Lifeguards are on duty during the summer season, mid-June to September. There are public restrooms just off the strip on West Grand Avenue.

Fees: Parking fee.

Scarborough Beach State Park

418 Black Point Road, Scarborough, ME

Sandy Scarborough Beach offers great swimming opportunities; however, there's a rip current here, so it's recommended that you swim in the designated swimming areas patrolled by lifeguards, on duty during the summer season, mid-June through Labor Day. Amenities include a concession stand, chair and umbrella rentals, showers, and restrooms.

Fees: Beach parking passes and boat-launching permits.

Pine Point Beach

Avenue 5, Scarborough, ME

A few miles north of Old Orchard Beach is Pine Point Beach in Scarborough, a long, sandy, family-oriented beach on Saco Bay that extends from the jetty at Pine Point to Old Orchard Beach. Amenities include a large parking lot, showers, restrooms, and concession stand. This is a popular beach for surf casting, surfing, and swimming. There are no lifeguards on duty at this beach.

Fees: Parking fee.

Higgins Beach

Bayview Avenue, Scarborough, ME

Higgins Beach is a sandy, half-mile-long beach, popular with surf casters and surfers. It's also a good place to hike along the shore, collecting shells and finding sand dollars. (Please don't collect the live sand dollars.) The beach is home to a shipwreck that is visible at low tide. Parking is available, but there are few amenities other than restrooms and an outdoor shower. There are no lifeguards on duty at this beach.

Fees: Parking fee.

Crescent Beach State Park

66 Two Lights Road, Cape Elizabeth, ME

Crescent Beach State Park in Cape Elizabeth is located eight miles south of Portland on Route 77. The mile-long beach is a popular location due to its gentle surf, and it's a great place for swimming, sunbathing, fishing, and kayaking. Amenities include a concession stand, picnic tables, bike racks, restrooms, cold-water showers, and plenty of parking. Lifeguards are on duty during the summer season, mid-June through Labor day.

Fees: Entrance fee to the park.

Willard Beach

South Portland, ME

Willard Beach in South Portland is a mile-long stretch of sand next to the oceanfront campus of Southern Maine Technical College. Fine sand and gentle surf make this a great summer destination, and it has all the requirements to be a good sea-glass beach. Amenities include restrooms, a concession stand, and parking. There are also other places to eat close by. Lifeguards are on duty during the summer season, mid-June to September.

East End Beach

Portland, ME

This small, rocky beach is located at the Eastern Promenade, with beautiful views of Portland Harbor. It is Portland's only public beach. Amenities include restrooms, changing rooms, and picnic tables, but there are no concession stands or snack bar, and no lifeguards on duty. Parking is limited. If you like to collect sea glass, this is a good spot to try.

Winslow Memorial Park

Staples Point Road, Freeport, ME

The park is operated by the town of Freeport and is home to a small tidal beach located between the Harraseeket River and Casco Bay. Amenities include restrooms, group shelters, campsites, picnic tables, playground, outdoor grills, a swimming platform, and a boat launch. There are no lifeguards on duty at this beach.
Fees: Camping and parking fees.

Thomas Point Beach

Meadow Road, Brunswick, ME

This is a privately owned park with a sandy beach that has just about everything. Amenities include a camping area, showers, picnic tables, playground, restrooms, and sports fields. The park is home to the Thomas Point Bluegrass Festival and the Maine Highland Games. There is so much to do here, the beach is almost an afterthought.
Fees: Entrance fee.

Popham Beach State Park

10 Perkins Farm Lane, Popham Beach, ME

Popham Beach is a large sandy beach located at the mouth of the Kennebec River, good for shell collecting. You should be a strong swimmer if you want to swim here, as Popham Beach is known for its strong surf and riptides. At low tide you can walk to Fox Island, but pay attention to the incoming tide, or you'll be stranded. Amenities include showers, picnic tables, charcoal grills, a bathhouse, and restroom facilities. Lifeguards are on duty daily during the summer season, mid-June through Labor Day.

Fees: Entrance fee.

Fowler Beach

Fowler Road, Long Island, Casco Bay, ME

This small sandy beach with its great views is located on Long Island in Casco Bay, and the best way to describe it from my visits is rocky, wet, and cold. There aren't any amenities, but hey, you're on an island in Maine. If you'd like to visit, you'll need to take the Casco Bay ferry from downtown Portland to the island. Once there, take Island Avenue to Jerry's Point Road to find this special beach.

Fees: Ferry ticket.

Reid State Park

375 Seguinland Road, Georgetown, ME

Reid State Park is home to Maine's first state-owned saltwater beach, and today, thousands of visitors enjoy the park's long, wide Mile and Half Mile sand beaches and the small rocky cove, known as East Beach. The beach is divided into three distinct beach sections, each with its own unique charm and beauty. Amenities include restrooms, a bathhouse, cold-water showers, restrooms, concession stands, showers, charcoal grills, and picnic areas. Climbing paths are found on the rock bluff, and this park is a prime location for bird watching. There are many tide pools and rocky areas that are great for sea life exploration. Lifeguards are on duty during the summer season, late June through Labor Day.

Fees: Entrance fee.

Colonial Pemaquid Beach

Route 130, Pemaquid, ME

This small sandy beach is ideal for those launching boats into Pemaquid Harbor; it's also a perfect place to launch your kayak. Immediately adjacent to the beach is a quaint restaurant with a deck and delicious food, as well as a small marina. Parking here is free, at the end of Colonial Pemaquid Road (off Snowball Hill Road, which connects from Route 130). Visit the fort next door during your beach trip.

Pemaquid Beach Park

Route 130, Pemaquid Point, ME

Pemaquid Beach is a quarter-mile-long, white-sand pocket beach located at Pemaquid Point that has consistently ranked as the cleanest beach in the state of Maine. The beach overlooks John's Bay and is owned by the town of Bristol. Amenities at this family-friendly beach include a concession stand, indoor and outdoor showers, changing rooms, beach chair and umbrella rentals, and an education center known as Beachcombers' Rest. There are no lifeguards on duty.

Fees: Entrance fee.

Birch Point State Park

South Shore Road, Owls Head, ME

Birch Point is an out-of-the-way classic pocket beach that offers solitude, a combination of cobbled and sandy, with rocky headlands on both sides. This is a good beach if you like geology, as the rocky areas are very interesting. Amenities include grills, picnic tables, restrooms, and plenty of parking. There are no lifeguards on duty at this beach.

Crocketts Beach

Crocketts Beach Road, Owls Head, ME

This small beach can be found off Ash Point Drive at the end of Crocketts Beach Road. There is no official parking at this beach, nor lifeguards or facilities.

Ash Point Beach

Ash Point Drive, Rockland, ME
Located on the corner of the West Penobscot Bay entryway, this small sand-and-rock beach has great views of the Gulf of Maine, including Dix Island Harbor, Vinalhaven, and North Haven. There is very limited parking, no facilities, and no lifeguards on duty.

Laite Memorial Beach

Bayview Street, Camden, ME
Laite Memorial Beach is a small, slightly cobbled beach located near Camden Harbor, a great place to go for a swim, look for beach glass, or just enjoy sitting and watching the boats as they enter and exit the harbor. The beach and park can be difficult to spot, but if you find Bayview Street, you should be able to find your way. Amenities include swings, picnic tables, restrooms, outdoor grills, and an outdoor shower. In the summer there's a raft for swimming. There are no lifeguards on duty at this beach, so you need to pay attention to your kids. We've had good luck hunting for sea glass at this beach.

Moose Point State Park

310 West Main Street, Searsport, ME
This park has lovely vistas, and is a great spot for tide-pool exploration. You can also have a cookout, as there are grills, picnic tables, and a covered pavilion available. This is not a swimming beach.
Fees: Entrance fee.

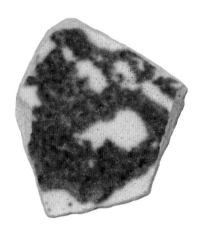

Fort Point State Historic Site

Off US Route 1, Stockton Springs, ME

This state park has about a mile of rocky, cobbled shoreline on Penobscot Bay. Amenities include grills, picnic tables, and restrooms. Although this isn't a swimming beach, it's a good place to look for sea glass.

Fees: Entrance fee.

Wadsworth Cove Beach

Back Shore Road, Castine, ME

This beach is located off Route 166 on Back Shore Road. It's made up of coarse sand and pebbles, but a good beach for kids, owing to its gentle surf. It's protected from rougher wave action because of its proximity to the Penobscot River. There are few amenities, and parking is along the street, but it does have an outhouse on-site.

Sand Beach

Park Loop Road, Acadia National Park, Mount Desert Island, ME

Sand Beach is a unique New England beach because of its composition: 80 percent, give or take, is ground-up shell matter, much of it from sea urchin shells. The water temperature is a balmy 50 to 60 degrees in summer, so you won't see a crowd of swimmers in the water, but it's a great place to spend the day. Amenities include changing rooms, restroom facilities, and ample parking. Lifeguards are on duty during the summer season, mid-June to Labor Day. If anyone becomes bored with the beach experience, they can walk across the street and climb the Beehive for a unique view of the beach and surrounding area. Heed the warning, though; the climb is not for the faint of heart, and children should always be supervised.

Fees: There is no beach fee, but you must pay an entrance fee to the National Park.

Little Hunters Beach

Park Loop Road, Acadia National Park, Mount Desert Island, ME

This small pocket beach is often overlooked by visitors to Acadia National Park, but is worth a stop if you can find a place to park. This is not a swimming beach, and there are no lifeguards. It has a strong undertow, so if you've come to the park to swim, you should go back around the Loop and stop at Sand Beach, where there are amenities and lifeguards. The reason to stop at Little Hunters is the millions of small pebbles that make up the shoreline and the rhythmic sound the waves make as the water drains through the rocky surface. It's the sound of tranquility. There are no amenities, with the exception of the wonderful sensory experience this beach offers.

Fees: There is no beach fee, but you must pay an entrance fee to the National Park.

Seawall

Seawall Road, Southwest Harbor, Mount Desert Island, ME

On the "quiet side," along Seawall Road and just in front of the Seawall Motel (say hi to David for me if you happen to stop in), is the beach. There are no amenities, but this long, arching, cobbled beach is a perfect location to view the sunrise, or sunset. Just down the road is a picnic area, and the often-photographed Bass Harbor Light. If you happen to visit the park, it's definitely worth a drive to this quiet, less-hectic section of Mount Desert Island.

Lamoine Beach

Lamoine Beach Road, Hancock, ME

Lamoine Beach is a good place for sea glass collecting and swimming. There are also picnic facilities available. Lamoine State Park is adjacent to the beach, and offers amenities as well, including outdoor grills, camping, showers, picnic table, restrooms, and a boat ramp for launching watercraft.

Fees: Entrance fee to the state park.

The Beach at Roque Bluffs State Park

145 Schoppee Point Road, Roque Bluffs, ME
The beach at this state park is a half-mile crescent of sand and pebbled shoreline. It's quiet, and a good place to hunt for tidal creatures and seashells. Amenities include parking, outhouse facilities, a children's playground, and a picnic area. There are no lifeguards at this beach.
Fees: Nominal parking fee.

Shackford Head

Off State Route 190, Eastport, ME
The park includes beaches, protected coves, and a bold headland. A hiking trail from the parking area offers great views of Cobscook Bay. This is not a swimming beach. Shackford Head is a great place for collecting beach stones and nature watching. Open year-round, sunrise to sunset. There are restroom facilities located near the parking lot.
Fees: Admission fee.

Red Beach

Route 1, Red Beach, ME

Red Beach is not a swimming beach, but is definitely worth a visit. It gets its name from the color of the granite outcroppings that contain a large amount of red feldspar. Because of its unique granite coloration, some of this stone was quarried in the 1800s for buildings and monuments along the East Coast, including the American Museum of Natural History in New York. Amenities include a boat ramp, restroom facilities, and a picnic area. Because this is not a swimming beach, no lifeguards are on duty.